For You, From Me

By
Raj Daniels

Copyright © 2017 Raj Daniels
All rights reserved.
ISBN: 1979093822
ISBN-13: 9781979093828

DEDICATION

Reyna, Ashna and Ariya. You inspire me to be better every day.

CONTENTS

1. ACKNOWLEDGMENTS 9
2. About the Book 10
3. Inspire Someone 12
4. What Are Your Values? 14
5. Your Calling 16
6. Small Changes 18
7. Highs and Lows 20
8. Your Way? 22
9. Relationship Budget 24
10. Is My Question Good Enough? 26
11. How Many? 28
12. Courage over Comfort 30
13. Bet on Yourself 32
14. Dumb Idea 34
15. ROI 36
16. Influence Your Thinking 38
17. Self-Care 40
18. The Invisible Cage 42
19. Not Good Enough 44
20. Why Can't You Be More Like? 46
21. The Wall 48
22. Re-Focus 50
23. If You Can't Say Something Nice 52

24.	A Little More	54
25.	Getting Even	56
26.	No Complaining	58
27.	You've Already Won	60
28.	Empty Space	62
29.	No Blueprint	64
30.	I Don't Know How To…	66
31.	Permission To Play	68
32.	Start to Start	70
33.	How Can I help You?	72
34.	Self-Worth	74
35.	A Good Person	76
36.	Need or Want?	78
37.	Why Am I Trying?	80
38.	Practice Makes You	82
39.	Be Sad	84
40.	Wish Others Happiness	86
41.	Unlimited Resources	88
42.	Superpower	90
43.	Break Your Routine	92
44.	The Idea Of	94
45.	You Don't Have To	96
46.	Time for You	98
47.	The Book About You	100
48.	Words	102

49. Better Than Yesterday 104
50. Diet & Exercise 106
51. Conventional Wisdom 108
52. What Are You Waiting For? 110
53. You Are Ignorant 112
54. Mistakes 114
55. 80% Silk 20% Cotton 116
56. Something from Nothing 118
57. I Don't Want To, But… 120
58. Weed, Water, Wait and Repeat 122
59. Stuff 124
60. The You of Tomorrow 126
61. Fingers Crossed 128
62. The Mover Advantage 130
63. Be Grateful 132
64. Your Natural Gifts 134
65. Handling Pressure and Stress 136
66. Energy for You 138
67. Give More 140
68. Anger 142
69. Show Yourself 144
70. Seed of Thought 146
71. What Matters to You? 148
72. I'm Proud of You 150
73. Your DNA 152

74. The End Comes After the Beginning 154
75. Measuring Progress 156
76. Be You 158
77. Build More Relationships 160
78. Stay Curious 162
79. Instant…Results? 164
80. Serendipitous Accidents 166
81. The Perfect Age 168
82. I Disagree 170
83. Uninterrupted Time 172
84. Blank Canvas 174
85. Discrepancy Syndrome 176
86. Your Emotions 178
87. Good News, Bad News 180
88. A Key to Learning 182
89. Mindless Accumulation 184
90. Take a Break from Media 186
91. Random Act of Kindness 188
92. A Penny for Your Thoughts 190
93. Make Someone's Day 192
94. FOMO 194
95. Perspective 196
96. Feeling Alive 198
97. Smiling and Dialing 200
98. Insecurity 202

99. Waiting for Permission	204
100. Your Last Words?	206
101. It's Messy for Everyone	208
102. One Size Fits One	210
103. Missing Pieces	212
104. Subconscious Choices	214
105. Infinite Loop	216
106. This Is It	218
107. Authors Note:	220

ACKNOWLEDGMENTS

To Juhy, Reyna, Ashna and Ariya a.k.a. my girls. Thank you for being the driving force behind all I do. Thank you Tom Calvaneso for showing up in my life when you did. Thank you Gary Keller for your Quantum Leap program which continues to greatly influence my thinking.

Thank you to the authors

Austin Kleon – Show Your Work

Seth Godin- What to Do When It's Your Turn

Steven Pressfield- The War of Art

It was in reading these books that finally pushed me over the edge to write my blog and Pressfield's continuous butt kicking of 'the resistance' that keeps me going.

And last but not least thank you to my parents Donald and Parin, for giving me life and saving my life.

Love always

Intentionally,

Raj

About the Book

This book is for you from me. It's not a book that's designed to be read from cover to cover, it's more of a conversation. You can move around the book as you wish as there is no real beginning or ending.

There are times when you're hungry for a meal and times when all you need is a snack, this book is that snack. The most frequent feedback I've received from the readers of my blog is that my posts serve as a small reminder about what's important, common sense or a quick dose of motivation to start their day. The posts are quickly digestible, 'snackable.'

There are 104 posts, 2 for each week of the year. Designed so that after each post you can capture your thoughts about what you read, any action you were inspired to take and what you learned after your action.

This book is for you to keep and reflect back on in the future. It's for you, from me.

Inspire Someone

Think of a time when you were inspired by words someone said to you.

How did it make you feel?

When was the last time you intentionally set out to inspire someone?

The word inspire originates from Latin and means breathe in or breath into, so when you inspire someone you breathe life into them. And how many people do you know that could use some inspiration?

A few simple inspirational words said with sincerity can make a huge difference in someone's day or even their life. So why not do it more often?

Inspiring someone will not cost you anything but your action will be priceless.

"If your actions inspire others to dream more, learn more, do more and become more, you are a leader."

-John Quincy Adams

For You, From Me

Date: _____

Thoughts_____
_____
_____
_____
_____
_____

Action_____
_____
_____
_____
_____
_____

Learn_____
_____
_____
_____
_____
_____

What Are Your Values?

Can you identify your values?

Have you ever thought about what your values are?

Your values describe what you believe in and how you will behave in certain situations. They provide you with a compass as you go through life. For example, if one of your core values is health then you will steer towards and prioritize healthy behavior.

You will know when you are not behaving in accordance with you values because you will experience feelings of guilt or remorse. You will feel out of sync with yourself.

Depending on your personality your values might change over time and that's okay since you're always encountering new information. And if changing benefits you and drives you towards your goals then that's great. However, if you change your values too often then there's a danger of feeling lost and not having any direction.

Taking some time to write down your values is great exercise because it will help you understand why you behave the way you do, and it will also help you better understand other people because you will learn that they are also behaving in alignment with their values.

"It's not hard to make decisions when you know what your values are."

-Roy E. Disney

For You, From Me

Date: _____

Thoughts _____
_____
_____
_____
_____
_____

Action _____
_____
_____
_____
_____
_____

Learn _____
_____
_____
_____
_____
_____

Your Calling

What is your calling?

What do you feel compelled to do?

What's the thing you hear or see other people doing that excites you?

I know these are big questions but they are really worth thinking about.

Somewhere inside you there are clues, little signals that are giving you messages about what you're interested in. Don't ignore them, explore them.

You don't have to start out by making a full-fledged commitment to any of your interests, you can dabble at will.

With all the resources available to you today a few hours of committed research can tell you so much about anything you feel you might be interested in doing.

The key to answering the big questions is giving yourself permission to look for the answers. When you find yourself drawn towards something that you think you might be interested in doing, don't smother the feeling, fuel it. You owe it to yourself and the world.

"There is no greater gift you can give or receive than to honor your calling. It's why you were born. And how you become most truly alive."

-Oprah

For You, From Me

Date: _____

Thoughts_____
_____
_____
_____
_____
_____

Action_____
_____
_____
_____
_____
_____

Learn_____
_____
_____
_____
_____
_____

Small Changes

What's the next thing about you that you plan on changing?

Oh, wait. You hadn't planned on changing anything? Well that's okay because change is going to happen anyway, regardless of if you're ready or not. So why not decide which changes you want to make?

You've probably heard that the only thing constant about life is change and this is so true, but what if all the changes weren't random. What if you could choose some of the changes?

Making big changes is a difficult endeavor because usually the bigger the change the longer it takes for you to adapt to it. One of the keys to making effective change is making a small change as possible. If you doubt that small change is effective then the next time you're driving turn the steering wheel just a little and see what happens.

When you get in the habit of intentionally making changes in your life you'll have a greater sense of control over yourself. And this sense of control will give you peace of mind and a feeling of power when you encounter external change.

"When you're finished changing, you're finished."
-Benjamin Franklin

For You, From Me

Date: _____

Thoughts _____
_____
_____
_____
_____
_____

Action _____
_____
_____
_____
_____
_____

Learn _____
_____
_____
_____
_____
_____

Highs and Lows

Imagine listening to a piece of music that only has high notes.

What would it sound like?

The beauty of high notes is clearer when they are contrasted with low notes and this same phenomenon applies to life too.

Every aspect of life has high and low notes and just like music it's the constant wave that that makes life enjoyable.

In your career, finances, health and relationships you will continuously experience highs and lows and it's because of the lows that you will enjoy the highs.

You may not see it but everyone is experiencing highs and lows on a continuous basis. The ones that don't seem to be affected by the lows are the ones that have learned to handle them or not show when they are experiencing them.

Just like music, the tempo of the highs and lows will constantly change, sometimes from minute to minute and other times it can be days. Enjoying and appreciating the highs when you are experiencing them, even if momentarily, will help you gain perspective when you experience the lows.

"Life is not linear; you have ups and downs. It's how you deal with the troughs that defines you."
-Michael Lee-Chin

For You, From Me

Date: _____

Thoughts_____
_____
_____
_____
_____
_____

Action_____
_____
_____
_____
_____
_____

Learn_____
_____
_____
_____
_____
_____

Your Way?

How much energy do you put in proving your way of doing something is right and others are wrong?

What do get from your effort and where did 'your way' come from?

When you choose to argue because you think you're right you are only doing so based on the information you believe to be correct and so is the other person. So, essentially you're both correct in in your own way.

If you research any profession you will find that even information that people have considered factual and founded on scientific evidence has changed over time based on new information.

Now there's a big difference between being correct and having a preference for how you want something to be, and when you realize this your life will change. It will change because you will no longer be attempting make the other person feel inferior for their preferences.

The question of being right or being happy is a popular one and perhaps your happiness is tied to you being right. However, that also means that you're invested in saying others are wrong. So the next time you find yourself in a situation where you're attempting to impose what you think is right ask yourself if you're really right or this is just your way and how you'd like things to be.

"Confidence comes not from always being right but from not fearing to be wrong."

-Peter Mcintyre

For You, From Me

Date: _____

Thoughts _____
_____
_____
_____
_____
_____

Action _____
_____
_____
_____
_____
_____

Learn _____
_____
_____
_____
_____
_____

Relationship Budget

What is your relationship budget?

Do you have one?

How do you allocate your time and energy to the people that mean the most to you? Do you give them the left over time you have at the end of the day or a week? Or do you prioritize them and invest in them frequently?

Relationships that aren't prioritized will naturally erode over time. The unfortunate thing is that they will dissolve not out of malice but lack of attention.

You wouldn't expect your bank account to magically accumulate money over time then don't expect the same from your relationships.

Invest intentionally in your relationships by being present and undistracted. You can choose how much time you want to invest based on your experience, and then get in the habit of setting aside that time to nurture the relationships that are important to you.

"You give but little when you give of your possessions. It is when you give of yourself that you truly give."

-Kahlil Gibran

For You, From Me

Date: _____

Thoughts_____

_____

_____

_____

_____

_____

Action_____

_____

_____

_____

_____

_____

Learn_____

_____

_____

_____

_____

_____

Is My Question Good Enough?

This is the question so many school children ask themselves before they raise their hands.

This is also a question that many adults ask themselves before opening their mouths because they don't want to look ill-informed or 'uneducated.'

This questioning the question is a debilitating action and will ultimately prevent you from growing past your current knowledge. However, there will be times when you will ask questions that some will consider being less than ideal or even stupid but that's okay as long as you are getting the answers you need.

It is very important that you don't confuse being shy with asking questions. Shy is a crutch that some individuals use to get out of asking questions. However, there are many that are socially shy or timid that have learned put aside their shyness in order to get answers to their questions.

Learning to ask questions is a muscle that can be strengthened over time and the more you practice the better you'll get. You can start practicing by asking questions that you already know the answer to. At least this way you'll feel more confident because you know you already have the answer.

"No one is dumb who is curious. The people who don't ask questions remain clueless throughout their lives."
-Neil deGrasse Tyson

For You, From Me

Date: _____

Thoughts _____
_____
_____
_____
_____
_____

Action _____
_____
_____
_____
_____
_____

Learn _____
_____
_____
_____
_____
_____

How Many?

How many more people do you have to read about that have done any of the following things?

Lost weight

Made money

Built great businesses

Donated to charity

Enjoyed their family

Lived their dreams

Written a book

Overcome adversity

Took their dream vacation

Reached their goals

How many more before you finally realize that they were no different from you? In fact, in some cases the individuals that have achieved their goals had none of the advantages you do.

Stop reading the press clippings of others and start writing your own. Write them down and then find a way to live into them. Make it your mission to not just to exist but to live!

"How many success stories do you need to hear before you make your own?"

−Unknown

For You, From Me

Date: _____

Thoughts _____

_____

_____

_____

_____

_____

Action _____

_____

_____

_____

_____

_____

Learn _____

_____

_____

_____

_____

_____

Courage over Comfort

Who's doing the thing you want to do?

Do you watch them from afar wishing it was you instead of them?

Do you see them acting, playing leading, writing, selling, building, loving and creating while you quietly envy them?

Why them and not you?

What makes them special?

What's holding you back from being that person?

There's only one difference between you and them. They identified what they wanted and then they found the courage to act on it. That's it. Simple yes, but definitely not easy.

So where is your courage?

Is it buried in your doubt?

Even the best, the individuals that are at the top of their chosen field have doubt, but they also have the magical power of acting despite their doubt.

Put aside you doubt today. Just for one day say and live with courage over comfort. Think of it as an experiment, and that you can always go back to being who you are.

"Choose courage over comfort."
—Brene Brown

For You, From Me

Date: _____

Thoughts _____
_____
_____
_____
_____
_____

Action _____
_____
_____
_____
_____
_____

Learn _____
_____
_____
_____
_____
_____

Bet on Yourself

Who are you going to bet on?

Are you betting on your boss, spouse, friends, family or your employees?

Who are you going to bet on to fulfill your dreams, wishes and desires?

If you decide to bet on anyone but yourself then essentially you are letting yourself off the hook. You are putting other people on a pedestal and saying that they are responsible for the results in your life.

Relinquishing responsibility for your own well-being is the easiest thing to do because it allows you to be the victim. It allows you to say 'it's not my fault,' and it allows you to get away with being less than your potential.

Learning to bet on you takes time and doesn't come naturally because it takes time to build the self-confidence to do so. However, if you take small steps and gather small wins then you will begin to experience a snowball effect in your own confidence ultimately allowing you take bigger bets on yourself.

Believe in yourself! Have faith in your abilities!

"Without a humble but reasonable confidence in your own powers you cannot be successful or happy."
-Norman Vincent Peale

For You, From Me

Date: _____

Thoughts_____

_____

_____

_____

_____

_____

Action_____

_____

_____

_____

_____

_____

Learn_____

_____

_____

_____

_____

_____

Dumb Idea

Have you ever had a dumb idea?

How did you know it was a dumb idea?

Did someone tell you or did you kill it before you shared it?

Are you familiar with the Chia Pet? It's been generating about $8,000,000 in revenue per year for 30 years. Or the Snuggie, which has sold over 30 million units and has generated about $500 million in gross revenue?

At first glance both of these ideas may have seemed like dumb ideas but both have proven quite the opposite.

Your own worst enemy when it comes to ideas is you. If you're like most then you probably hesitate in sharing your ideas because you fear looking inept, unqualified or even dumb. And the truth is that sometimes you will and that's okay.

Learn to share your ideas more freely. Get in the practice of writing them down and exploring them a little further. Some of your ideas may truly sound dumb at first, but don't forget that even the Pet Rock made $6 million in profits.

"Not to engage in the pursuit of ideas is to live like ants instead of like men."

-Mortimer Adler

For You, From Me

Date: _____

Thoughts_____
_____
_____
_____
_____
_____

Action_____
_____
_____
_____
_____
_____

Learn_____
_____
_____
_____
_____
_____

ROI

What do you expect from the time you invest in a relationship?

What do you expect from the love you invest in your children?

What do you expect from the money you invest in a business or the stock market?

What do you expect from the investment in your health?

What do you expect from all of your investments? What do you expect from them and what happens to you after you make the investments?

The good news and the bad news is the returns you expect are rarely the returns you get. Sometimes you're up and sometimes you're down.

Does this mean you shouldn't invest time, emotions and money? Well, it might. And that will depend on your tolerance for uncertainty and how you respond when things don't go as expected.

If returns and results were guaranteed in any area of life then the world would be perfect, and boring. The one guaranteed return from your investments will be your experience. And how you respond to the experience will dictate your future investments.

"The only certainty is that nothing is certain."
-Pliny the Elder

For You, From Me

Date: _____

Thoughts_____
_____
_____
_____
_____
_____

Action_____
_____
_____
_____
_____
_____

Learn_____
_____
_____
_____
_____
_____

Influence Your Thinking

Who or what do you think influences how you think, family, friends, the media? Your thoughts are influenced by whatever you put your attention on. So whatever you expose yourself to on a daily basis will overtime drive your thinking, whether you admit it or not.

Your brain absorbs so much information in a subliminal manner and you're often unaware of all the information being stored. That's why advertisers keep showing and playing the same ads over and over, because they know that even though you think you're ignoring them, your brain is in fact storing them.

There will be times when you cannot avoid information or stories that lead you to think about things that bring you down. However, if you want to experience strong, positive uplifting thoughts then you should make a conscious effort to expose your mind to information that will help you lead such a life.

"The mind is everything. What you think you become."
-Buddha

For You, From Me

Date: _____

Thoughts _____
_____
_____
_____
_____
_____

Action _____
_____
_____
_____
_____
_____

Learn _____
_____
_____
_____
_____
_____

Self-Care

Do you have a self-care program?

A system where you take time to prioritize yourself or have you chosen to sacrifice your well-being for others?

You're probably familiar with the overplayed airline message of 'put on your own mask before attempting to help others,' but there is so much truth to this.

If you don't take invest time in self-care then not only are you less effective for yourself, but also towards those whom you want to help.

When you prioritize caring for yourself not only will you benefit mentally and physically, you will also reap psychological and emotional benefits too.

Self-care doesn't have to consist of hours of self-indulgence; it can be accomplished in just a few minutes a day. A few minutes set aside to breathe, to think, to move, to eat right all in order to replenish and rejuvenate your mind and body which will ultimately do wonders for you.

"Self-care is not selfish. You cannot serve from an empty vessel."
-Eleanor Brownn

For You, From Me

Date: _____

Thoughts _____
_____
_____
_____
_____
_____

Action _____
_____
_____
_____
_____
_____

Learn _____
_____
_____
_____
_____
_____

The Invisible Cage

How do you escape from an invisible cage?

If you can't see it then how do you know it exists?

Well, there's proof it does exist.

And the proof is in the feeling you get when you hear the little voice in your head say "what will they think?"

Does it sound familiar?

If you listen carefully you can hear it right now.

It's warming up for the day, just waiting for you to think about doing something. That's right, you just have to think about doing something and the voice will jump in to action.

You will hear it in its full authority.

"You're going to wear that?" "What will they think?"

"You're going say that?" "What will they think?"

"You're going to do that?" "What will they think?"

And over time each time the voice says "what will they think?" another bar of the invisible cage will seal your fate. Until finally your entire existence will be based on 'what will they think.'

And one day you'll wake up and realize they weren't thinking about you at all, because they were too busy thinking about themselves and what you think about them.

"What other people think of you is none of your business."

-Regina Brett

For You, From Me

Date: _____

Thoughts _____
_____
_____
_____
_____
_____

Action _____
_____
_____
_____
_____

Learn _____
_____
_____
_____
_____

Not Good Enough

Do you hesitate to try something new because you think you're 'not good enough?'

Well, you're probably right, and that's okay.

The feeling of not being good enough to even try something is like an invisible cage that prevents you from experiencing new and exciting things. And the thing about this feeling is that it never goes away, it will be there every time you think about trying something new or different.

The trick is to embrace the feeling, acknowledge that you're not good enough and that is exactly why you are going to move forward realizing all the while that even when you get better you'll still feel as though you're not good enough.

Don't let the feeling of not being good enough hold you back. The truth is you're already good enough to start anything.

"You are good enough, until you get better."

-Suriya

For You, From Me

Date: _____

Thoughts_____

_____
_____
_____
_____
_____

Action_____

_____
_____
_____
_____
_____

Learn_____

_____
_____
_____
_____
_____

Why Can't You Be More Like?

Has anyone ever asked you, why you can't be more like someone else?

Was it a parent, spouse, employer or friend that asked you? How did it make you feel?

Did the question make you feel inadequate and question yourself? Or were you able to shrug of their question and remain confident in who you are?

The ability to remain resilient to a world that is constantly telling you how you should be is a skill that can serve you well. This is not to say that you shouldn't model other people if it serves you in achieving your goals, but don't forget that even those you attempt to imitate have flaws that you'll never see.

Remaining strong in your endeavor to be yourself regardless of the constant pressure to be someone else will serve you well over the long term. And the world will benefit from your uniqueness, not you trying to be someone else.

"When you are content to be simply yourself and don't compare or compete, everybody will respect you."

-Lao Tzu

For You, From Me

Date: _____

Thoughts_____
_____
_____
_____
_____
_____

Action_____
_____
_____
_____
_____
_____

Learn_____
_____
_____
_____
_____
_____

The Wall

What will you do when you hit a wall? Not a physical wall, but a metaphorical wall?

When you hit a wall in your relationship will your first thought be, how can I get out of this?

When hit you hit a wall in your career will your first instinct be submission?

When you hit a wall in your health will you give up on yourself?

The wall in any aspect of your life is inevitable. Think of the wall as the fall when you learned to walk. Imagine if you had given up on your first attempt.

The size of the wall will be relative to the size of what you are trying to accomplish. Almost anyone can hop over a single brick but only some have the skills and resourcefulness to overcome the big daunting walls.

How you think about the wall will determine your approach. If you see it as a dead end then that's what it will be. However, if you see it as part of your journey to a worthwhile destination then your approach will be different and you'll find a way to overcome it.

"Obstacles don't have to stop you. If you run into a wall, don't turn around and give up. Figure out how to climb it, go through it, or work around it."

-Michael Jordan

For You, From Me

Date: _____

Thoughts_____
_____
_____
_____
_____
_____

Action_____
_____
_____
_____
_____
_____

Learn_____
_____
_____
_____
_____
_____

Re-Focus

How will you see the world today?

What will you decide to put your attention on?

Will you start your day reading or listening to the news telling you about all the bad things going on in the world?

Will you focus on the traffic, the construction, the 'bad weather?'

Will you be looking for faults in people around you?

Will you think about all the things you don't have?

Or will you decide to re-focus and drive your attention towards all that is good around you and be grateful for what you do have?

Your attention is focused awareness, and with practice you can train yourself to ignore things in your surroundings that you can't change and focus on the things you can.

Try an experiment today. When you find yourself complaining or thinking about something negative that you have no control over, quickly re-focus to something positive in your life.

Over time and with practice this will become easier as you re-wire your brain to your new habit and soon enough you will find this will be your new natural state.

"What you focus on grows, what you think about expands, and what you dwell upon determines your destiny."

-Robin Sharma

For You, From Me

Date: _____

Thoughts_____
_____
_____
_____
_____
_____

Action_____
_____
_____
_____
_____

Learn_____
_____
_____
_____
_____
_____

If You Can't Say Something Nice

What if it were your job to only say good things about people?

What if your success and happiness in life depended on the words you use to describe your family, friends, acquaintances etc.?

If this were true, who would you choose to be around, and would you change your thinking and language towards them?

What does shining a light on some ones assumed shortcomings say about you? I say assumed because you never truly know the reason an individual is behaving the way they are.

As a kid you probably heard 'if you can't say something nice then don't say nothing at all,' and there is truth in this.

So, the next time you speak about someone, be aware of what you're going to say, and if it's not nice then consider refraining because what you're about to say is as much a reflection on you as it is about them.

"If you can't say something nice then don't say nothing at all."
-Thumper

Date: _____

Thoughts _____
_____
_____
_____
_____
_____

Action _____
_____
_____
_____
_____
_____

Learn _____
_____
_____
_____
_____
_____

A Little More

When was the last time you pushed yourself just a little more, physically or intellectually?

Pushing yourself to do a little more is your key to personal growth because it gives you confidence that you control your mind and that you can reach beyond your current capacity.

Doing a little more can be a simple as adding an extra minute to your exercise routine, reading an additional page of a book or spending a few minutes researching or learning about something that you're working on.

The power behind doing a little more is that your efforts compound over time and your ability to control your mindset of being able to do a little more is a transferable skill.

Make an effort today to do just a little more than you think you can and notice how you feel a sense of pride as you realize just how much power you actually have over yourself.

"A little more persistence, a little more effort, and what seemed hopeless failure may turn to glorious success."
-Elbert Hubbard

For You, From Me

Date: _____

Thoughts _____
_____
_____
_____
_____
_____

Action _____
_____
_____
_____
_____
_____

Learn _____
_____
_____
_____
_____
_____

Getting Even

What do you do when someone treats you poorly?

Do you spend your time and energy thinking of ways to return the sentiment?

Do you say things like, if that's' how they behave then I'm going to respond in a similar manner? Do you become more like them?

If you have a set of guiding principles that you believe in for your own life then why would you compromise them based on someone else's actions. Yes, it can be easy in the moment to react with a, I'm going to show them attitude, but where does that get you.

Not responding when you feel attacked or slighted is difficult because your ego jumps in to protect your identity. But if you're confident in your identity then why does it matter what someone else says to or about you?

Don't spend your precious life dwelling on or thinking about what people have said and done that has hurt or offended you. Instead, refocus and think about all the people that have been kind and thoughtful towards you, and you'll see that your life will be much brighter.

"The ones that you should try to get even with are the ones who have helped you."
-Unknown

For You, From Me

Date: _____

Thoughts_____
_____
_____
_____
_____
_____

Action_____
_____
_____
_____
_____
_____

Learn_____
_____
_____
_____
_____
_____

No Complaining

Do you complain about things you can't change, things that you have no control over?

Why do you do this? Does it make you feel better or change the situation?

Do you complain about?

The weather

The traffic

Your coworkers

Your family

The news

The economy

Or do you have any other personal favorites?

Complaining puts things you don't like into greater focus which in turn makes the thing you're complaining about seem more relevant than it is.

What if today you made the choice not to complain about the things you can't change? And instead of complaining you just re-focused your mind.

When you find yourself complaining about something that you have no control over, learn to get in the habit of quickly changing your thoughts towards something you're grateful for. By practicing this over time you won't even notice the things you once complained about.

"Be grateful for what you have and stop complaining - it bores everybody else, does you no good, and doesn't solve any problems."
- Zig Ziglar

Date: _____

Thoughts_____
_____
_____
_____
_____

Action_____
_____
_____
_____
_____

Learn_____
_____
_____
_____

You've Already Won

If you're reading this then you've already won.

Why have you won?

You've won because:

You know how to read.

You have the time to read.

You have a device to read on.

You can afford your device.

You have the command of the powerful language in the world. Yes, the majority of all worldwide business communication is conducted in English.

So now that you know that you've already won, what will you do with your winnings?

Will you squander all your time and skills on trivial activities that waste away all that you've already won, or will you build a life of opportunities?

The choice is yours.

"Take what you have and make what you want."

-Suriya

For You, From Me

Date: _____

Thoughts_____
_____
_____
_____
_____
_____

Action_____
_____
_____
_____
_____
_____

Learn_____
_____
_____
_____
_____
_____

Empty Space

How often do you leave space in your life for magic to happen, to experience serendipitous interactions and opportunities?

Living with your days crammed with activities and things to do leave you with little or no room for 'by chance encounters.'

You don't have to schedule hours of empty space but you do have to make an effort to make time for opportunity. You can do something as simple as go to a coffee shop and talk to a stranger with no agenda or outcome in mind. You can take a walk without listening to music or talking on phone, just looking and absorbing your environment.

There are numerous examples in history, such as Newton and his apple or Archimedes and his bathtub where inspiration for a new idea struck when least expected because of empty space.

Make it a practice to add, or perhaps better said, to remove constant activity and input to your life. Leave some empty space for yourself and see what magic you experience.

"Make an empty space in any corner of your mind, and creativity will instantly fill it."
-Dee Hock

For You, From Me

Date: _____

Thoughts _____
_____
_____
_____
_____
_____

Action _____
_____
_____
_____
_____
_____

Learn _____
_____
_____
_____
_____
_____

No Blueprint

Are you trying to follow a blueprint of someone else's life to fix or improve your own life?

The problem with blueprints, templates and other such mechanical terms is that they only work for mechanical objects.

Take a diet for example. A 100 people could be on the same diet down to the last calorie counted and measured, and yet there would be 100 different results because no two individuals are the same.

When you find yourself saying, but it worked for her or that's how he did it, you are inviting yourself down a slippery road. You are making the error of assuming you are the same as the other person.

Now there are guidelines you can use to direct your life and they can help you move in the general direction towards what you want to accomplish but guidelines don't guarantee 'success.'

Someone else's life blueprint can be a good starting point for you, but only as learning tool for you to continue to conduct your own life experiment and find a way to be a unique, original you.

"Don't be a blueprint. Be an original."
-Roy Acuff

For You, From Me

Date: _____

Thoughts_____
_____
_____
_____
_____
_____

Action_____
_____
_____
_____
_____
_____

Learn_____
_____
_____
_____
_____
_____

I Don't Know How To...

Do you let not knowing how to do something stop you from moving forward?

When you have a thought or dream of doing something new does your mind answer with 'but I don't know how,' and you stop before you start?

Yes, there is uncertainty in feeling that you don't know how to do something, but it can also be liberating.

Learn to develop the perspective that not knowing how to do something is a great position to be in. It means that your options are wide open and you have the freedom to experiment without any preconceived notions of the 'right way.'

Don't let not knowing how be your crutch that you fall back on and stop you from moving forward.

You live in a world of abundant resources and the answer to almost every one of your 'don't know hows' can be found as long as you are willing to look for them. And for the answers you can't find, well now you have the opportunity to be the one with answer to someone else's 'I don't know how.'

"Being at ease with not knowing is crucial for answers to come to you."
-Eckhart Tolle

For You, From Me

Date: _____

Thoughts _____
_____
_____
_____
_____
_____

Action _____
_____
_____
_____
_____
_____

Learn _____
_____
_____
_____
_____
_____

Permission To Play

Do you give yourself permission to play; to lose yourself in an activity that you enjoy so much that time disappears?

It's been said, play is essential to creativity. Playing enables your imagination to express itself in ways you wouldn't normally do in your everyday routines.

Playing is different for everyone and there are no set guidelines for the correct way to play. Playing for you could mean participating in sporting activities, wrestling with children or just watching movies.

As an adult you will always have 'adult' responsibilities as part of life and they will never go away. But that doesn't mean you shouldn't give yourself permission to play.

Indulge yourself occasionally in guilt free play time and don't worry about all the other adult stuff, it'll still be there when you're done playing.

"In every real man a child is hidden that wants to play."
-Friedrich Nietzsche

For You, From Me

Date: _____

Thoughts_____
_____
_____
_____
_____
_____

Action_____
_____
_____
_____
_____
_____

Learn_____
_____
_____
_____
_____
_____

Start to Start

What personal project, goal or idea have you been putting off?

What's that one thing that you think about that you really want to do that you haven't taken any action on? It could be as small as clean the junk draw or as big as travelling the world.

What's yours?

Make time today to write down one thing you want to do. And I don't mean make a list or take a note. Write it out in long form and go in to as much detail as possible. Describe what the end result will look like and what it will mean to you.

Starting is one of the best habits you can develop for yourself. Not only will you get more done but it's only after starting that you can really grasp the effort required in accomplishing what you want and it will also help you decide if you really want to continue.

"To achieve greatness, start where you are, use what you have, do what you can."

–Arthur Ashe

For You, From Me

Date: _____

Thoughts _____
_____
_____
_____
_____
_____

Action _____
_____
_____
_____
_____
_____

Learn _____
_____
_____
_____
_____
_____

How Can I help You?

How can I help you?

How may I serve you?

What can I do for you?

These questions have magic within them. They have the power to transform your life if you ask them with a sincere desire to serve others.

These questions also require you to have an abundance mindset because you have to know that you have enough time, energy and mental capacity in order to make time to do things for other people.

Research shows, when you help others you'll receive the added benefit of feeling good about yourself too.

So make helping others part of your daily routine. Add these questions to your vocabulary, make a habit of using them often, and experience how your life changes when you commit to helping others.

"You will get all you want in life, if you help enough other people get what they want."

–Zig Ziglar

For You, From Me

Date: _____

Thoughts_____
_____
_____
_____
_____
_____

Action_____
_____
_____
_____
_____
_____

Learn_____
_____
_____
_____
_____
_____

Self-Worth

What is your self-worth tied to?

Is it tied to the amount of money you make, the number material possessions you have, your house, your car, your job, where you live? Would you have less self-worth if you lost any of the preceding items? Is it tied to how people see you? What if they were no longer in your life?

Self-worth begins from respecting yourself. It starts with appreciating who you are regardless of what you have. Now this sounds easy but you'll be challenged daily by external forces such as family, friends, media and advertising telling you that you're not worthy until you have, what they think is important.

Fighting these external forces is tough and you'll often find yourself second guessing your self-worth because you begin to assess your value through the eyes of others. And you begin to measure yourself against other people.

The first steps to improving your self-worth are to stop tying your self-worth to possessions and to stop comparing yourself to others. Comparing yourself to others is not only destructive but it doesn't make logical sense since each individual is made from a totally different set of DNA.

When you find yourself questioning your self-worth, challenge your inner thoughts, see yourself for who you are and commit to appreciating who you are and what you have.

"Self-worth comes from one thing - thinking that you are worthy."
-Wayne Dyer

Date: _____

Thoughts_____
_____
_____
_____
_____

Action_____
_____
_____
_____
_____

Learn_____
_____
_____
_____
_____

A Good Person

Are you a good person?

I was at dinner with a friend and she shared that she was interviewing her grandmother and one of her questions to her grandmother was 'do you have any advice for your grandchildren?' And her grandmother had one answer, be a good person.

It's not the first time I've heard this, especially from people who are in the later years of their lives. The people that have lived the longest seem to realize that in the end once you strip away all the titles, money, awards and material possessions very little really matters except being a good person.

So what if you start off with the end in mind of being known as a good person?

What if you made that your guiding light? How would you live your life? How would your priorities change? Would you behave differently?

Being a good person is a broad definition and can mean different things to people, however there are some key characteristics that most can agree on. If being a good person is important to you then start working on the behavior that will result on you being a known, as a good person.

"Be a good person."
–Wise old people

For You, From Me

Date: _____

Thoughts_____
_____
_____
_____
_____
_____

Action_____
_____
_____
_____
_____
_____

Learn_____
_____
_____
_____
_____
_____

Need or Want?

What are the things in life you need and what are the ones you want?

Finding a balance between the two can be challenging especially if you have trouble differentiating wants and needs.

Food/water, shelter and clothing were at one time considered basic needs and more recently sanitation, education and healthcare were added to the list. Now each one of these categories is vast and can span the spectrum from very basic to highly sophisticated.

Differentiating between a need and want can be tricky because the language seems to be interchangeable and external influences often lead you to believe wants are needs. The key is for you to use the language correctly.

Having wants is good in that it can push you and motivate you towards certain goals. But just remember, because you want something doesn't mean you need it.

"The difference between want and need is self-control."
-Unkown

For You, From Me

Date: _____

Thoughts_____
_____
_____
_____
_____
_____

Action_____
_____
_____
_____
_____
_____

Learn_____
_____
_____
_____
_____
_____

Why Am I Trying?

Have you ever asked yourself, why am I even trying?

Why am I even trying to be happy, lose weight, earn more money, be in a relationship, build a business or any other endeavor?

The why am I trying question usually arises when whatever you're attempting to do seems impossible. Or when you think it's just way too hard to continue. And it can be a very valid question. However, in the question lies the answer.

It's in the 'why?'

What is your motivation for trying?

What will you gain, what will you become if you succeed and will you be strong enough and willing enough to pay the price?

Defining your reasons for why to start and also re-examining your why while you're on your journey will help you decide if you should continue. The majority of people that quit going after what they want is because they stop asking why.

Keep your why in front of you. Read it or see it on a regular basis so that when things do get difficult, you will know why you are trying.

"What win I, if I gain the thing I seek?"
-Shakespeare

For You, From Me

Date: _____

Thoughts _____
_____
_____
_____
_____
_____

Action _____
_____
_____
_____
_____

Learn _____
_____
_____
_____
_____
_____

Practice Makes You

What do you think of when you hear the word practice?

Do you think of athletes, musicians, even perhaps religion or some other activity that requires repeated attention in order to improve?

And you would be correct to think so, but what about you?

What do you practice?

When you see an athlete or performer practicing they are engaging in an intentional activity to improve their ability to perform. The same applies to you except you're usually thinking or doing without being intentional, because it's just how you are. Or is it?

When an athlete sees that something is no longer working for them they work to change to it, they practice something new.

What about you?

Every behavior you perform on a regular basis regardless of it being positive or negative is a practice. It's just that you don't view it as practice or re-affirming, you just see it as who you are. The reason the athlete is motivated to change their behavior and practice something new is because their livelihood depends on it. The same should apply to you too, because ultimately your life depends on it too.

"You are what you practice most."
–Richard Carlson

For You, From Me

Date: _____

Thoughts_____
_____
_____
_____
_____
_____

Action_____
_____
_____
_____
_____
_____

Learn_____
_____
_____
_____
_____
_____

Be Sad

Be sad.

That's right, be sad, embrace your feeling of melancholy and give yourself permission to explore why you're feeling sad.

With so much focus on being happy, sadness is shunned as a bad emotion. However, as a human you're designed to feel sadness. The key is how you deal with it.

Any emotion, positive or negative, requires a high level of effort and energy to maintain over a long period of time because you are constantly looking for reasons to justify feeling the emotion, to validate your feelings.

Don't be afraid of sharing that you're feeling sad. Those that really care for you will understand and you'll also give them permission to share when they're feeling sad too.

While experiencing sadness is part of part of life, you do not need to dwell on it. Experience it, understand it, and then re-focus on the things that do make you happy and that you are grateful for. Allowing yourself to feel the range of emotions that you were made to feel is an integral part of the human experience.

"The word 'happy' would lose its meaning if it were not balanced by sadness."

-Carl Jung

For You, From Me

Date: _____

Thoughts _____
_____
_____
_____
_____
_____

Action _____
_____
_____
_____
_____
_____

Learn _____
_____
_____
_____
_____
_____

Wish Others Happiness

Do you spend any of your time consciously wishing others well?

Wishing them happiness and sending them good thoughts?

Or are you so focused inward that the well-being, happiness and success of others never crosses your mind?

Wishing others happiness is not a natural behavior for everyone, but it can be learned with practice. I know you might be thinking 'what if someone has done something to hurt or betray you, how can you wish them happiness?' And this is a valid question. But how much time and energy can you spend being upset with them and what was your role in the situation?

Wishing others happiness can actually improve how you feel about yourself because it shifts your mind, even if temporarily from thinking about your own problems and challenges.

Practice today to send thoughts of happiness to people you know and random strangers and experience how it changes your day.

"Wishing people well does not define them, it defines you."
-Suriya

For You, From Me

Date: _____

Thoughts_____
_____
_____
_____
_____
_____

Action_____
_____
_____
_____
_____
_____

Learn_____
_____
_____
_____
_____
_____

Unlimited Resources

If you had unlimited time, money and energy what would you do with your life?

Would you really be motivated to do anything productive?

Working within resource constraints naturally forces you to be more creative. It pushes your mind to find new and unique ways to produce results. Nature itself is designed to work and produce against constrained conditions and the strongest of any species are those that learn to adapt and thrive with limited resources.

Nothing you need to or want to start doing requires unlimited resources; in fact having limited resources forces you to be more resourceful. Whatever you want to do, start today and remember, the only place you need to have unlimited resources is in your mind.

"Whom the gods wish to destroy, they give unlimited resources."
-Twyla Tharp

For You, From Me

Date: _____

Thoughts_____
_____
_____
_____
_____
_____

Action_____
_____
_____
_____
_____
_____

Learn_____
_____
_____
_____
_____
_____

Superpower

What is your super power?

The thing that you are so good at that you always feel confident when you do it?

The skill that when you look back on your life you know you could always rely on?

If you don't know, or are not sure what your super power is then think of a time when someone asked you 'how do you that? You're so good at that? Or, 'that comes so easily to you? These are all clues to what your super power is. You can also think about activities you really enjoy doing, productive activities that you would do for free.

Once you identify your super power then you can learn to nurture and grow it. You can design your life around it. You can find roles or jobs that leverage your inherent talent and when you do you will ultimately do and feel better.

"Focus on your strengths instead of your weaknesses, on your powers instead of your problems."
-Paul J. Meyer

For You, From Me

Date: _____

Thoughts_____
_____
_____
_____
_____
_____

Action_____
_____
_____
_____
_____
_____

Learn_____
_____
_____
_____
_____
_____

Break Your Routine

Break one of your routines today.

Choose one thing you find yourself doing every day and change it just for today.

It doesn't have to be huge change; in fact it can be a small as using a different cup for coffee, using the opposite hand to brush your teeth or sitting somewhere else at work. Just something that feels a little different.

Making a small change to a routine will engage a different part of your brain and spark new connections. You'll see the world differently and experience different emotions.

Breaking a routine can be a great gateway for creating new habits. It can give you the courage to eventually make bigger more drastic changes because you learn to get comfortable with change.

Try it today, because you have nothing to lose. If you don't like the change you can always go back to your routine.

"Chains of habit are too light to be felt until they are too heavy to be broken."

-Warren Buffett

Date: _____

Thoughts_____
_____
_____
_____
_____
_____

Action_____
_____
_____
_____
_____
_____

Learn_____
_____
_____
_____
_____
_____

The Idea Of

Do you like the idea of being happy?

Do you like the idea of being healthy or the idea of being wealthy?

The idea of being in a relationship or any other endeavor?

While taking a walk one morning I saw a man walking a large black and white Old English sheepdog. Now if you've ever seen one of these dogs you know that they are beautiful and for a quick minute my mind wandered to the idea of owning such a dog. But very quickly I realized that I liked the idea, but not the work and maintenance that's required in owning one.

Falling in to the trap of liking the idea of something is very easy to do because your mind rushes to the end product, the picture of how your life would look. And there's nothing wrong with imagining how you want your life to look. In fact it's the starting point of all great journeys.

The key is to realize that every end product, every idea and dream realized is going to take a lot of work and very often more work than you realized. It's going to take work to start, to continue and to maintain and just liking the 'idea of' will not get you there.

"Ideas don't work unless you do the work."
-Robin Sharma

For You, From Me

Date: _____

Thoughts _____
_____
_____
_____
_____
_____

Action _____
_____
_____
_____
_____
_____

Learn _____
_____
_____
_____
_____
_____

You Don't Have To

Do you believe that you have to behave the way you do?

That you have to respond and react the way you do?

That there's no other way for you?

Do you have to yell at your spouse or children when you are upset?

Do you have to eat the unhealthy food because it's there in front of you?

Do you have to check your email or social media one more time just in case you miss something?

Do you have to have wander aimlessly through life being the victim of your circumstances?

Do you have to…fill in your own have to?

If you believe that you have to do any of the items above then you fallen in to a trap. Because everything you see listed here is something you learned to do. At some point in your life you adopted a mindset or a behavior because you thought this is how I need to behave. But you don't have to. You choose to.

If you want to act a certain way then at least own the behavior and don't blame it on 'have to.'

When you do step up and own your behavior is when you have the opportunity to change it… if you choose to, but you don't have to.

"Be miserable. Or motivate yourself. Whatever has to be done, it's always your choice."
-Wayne Dyer

Date: _____

Thoughts_____
_____
_____
_____
_____

Action_____
_____
_____
_____
_____

Learn_____
_____
_____
_____
_____

Time for You

Do you schedule time with yourself to do the things are important to you?

Or do you rely on an ad hoc; I'll just get to me when I can system?

Giving all your time to your work and family might seem noble at first, however it will cause you to feel out of control and over time build up feelings of resentment for both.

Prioritizing a little of your time for yourself lets you know you too are important and you're not just living a reactive life. It doesn't have to be a lot of time, even a few minutes a day can make a big difference to how you feel.

Look at your calendar today and schedule a few minutes for yourself tomorrow and treat that time just as you would any other appointment.

"Guard your time fiercely. Be generous with it, but be intentional about it."
–David Duchemin

For You, From Me

Date: _____

Thoughts _____
_____
_____
_____
_____
_____

Action _____
_____
_____
_____
_____
_____

Learn _____
_____
_____
_____
_____
_____

The Book About You

If someone wrote a book about you how would they describe you?

If they interviewed your family and friends for the book what would they say about how you treated people? Would they say you were kind, generous, caring, optimistic and uplifting? The kind of person that people would say it was a pleasure to be around.

Or would they write that you were always complaining, gossiping, quick to find fault in others, pessimistic, demeaning? The kind of person that people went out of their way to avoid being around.

The book about you is being written by you on daily basis and every interaction is an opportunity for you decide now, what want you want to be written in the future book about you.

"What you leave behind is not what is engraved on stone monuments, but what is woven into the lives of others."
—Pericles

For You, From Me

Date: _____

Thoughts_____
_____
_____
_____
_____
_____

Action_____
_____
_____
_____
_____

Learn_____
_____
_____
_____
_____

Words

What words do you use do describe yourself?

What words do you use to describe the kind of day you're having?

What words do you use to describe how you feel?

Your words are the palette for your thoughts and actions. They can color your day by adding excitement and enthusiasm or they can bring feelings of despair and sadness.

The vocabulary you use can also directly affect how you feel about yourself and others. It can also affect how others see you. Research shows that individuals can actually alter not just their psychology but also physiology just by the words they use.

Every thought you have is labeled with a word. Your thoughts are strings of words constantly churning through your brain sending signals on how you should act and feel. Your entire perspective of the world is based on the words that you're in the habit of using.

Learn to use strong, powerful, uplifting words to describe yourself and positive words to describe your relationships and people around you. Your words can change the lens through which you view and live your life, choose them wisely.

"Change your words, change your life."
–Tony Robbins

For You, From Me

Date: _____

Thoughts_____
_____
_____
_____
_____
_____

Action_____
_____
_____
_____
_____
_____

Learn_____
_____
_____
_____
_____
_____

Better Than Yesterday

Are you better in any area of life today than you were yesterday?

If yesterday is too soon then how about last week, last month or last year?

If not, then why not? Is it that you don't believe in self-improvement or do you think it will just happen by itself?

Self-improvement doesn't have to be a daunting task or come in the form of a drastic change. In fact small incremental changes that are barely noticeable have the power to accumulate over time and are very often more effective because they allow you to adjust to your new state of being.

Self-improvement also doesn't mean that you're not happy, appreciative or accepting where you are right now but it does mean that you understand that you if you're not moving forward in the important areas of your life then you are indeed moving backwards.

The areas of life you should look for continuous improvement in are, family/relationships, career/finance, health/physical and religious/spiritual.

Write down one small, tiny little thing you'd like to improve in each area and think about it for a few days. Imagine how your life would be different if you committed to taking the steps that would make you better than yesterday.

"Without continual growth and progress, such words as improvement, achievement, and success have no meaning."

-Benjamin Franklin

For You, From Me

Date: _____

Thoughts_____
_____
_____
_____
_____
_____
_____

Action_____
_____
_____
_____
_____
_____
_____

Learn_____
_____
_____
_____
_____
_____
_____

Diet & Exercise

I know what you're thinking. You're thinking Raj must be running out of ideas to write about and that you can skip this post because you already know all there is to know about diet and exercise. And you're right; you can skip this post because like the majority of people you do know about diet and exercise.

But before you go let me share something you might not know. The weight loss industry is a $64 Billion dollar market!

So, if you and the majority of people know about diet & exercise then why is the market so big and still growing? It's because the majority of people are looking for the 'quick fix.' They're looking for the 7 day, 30 day, or even the 1 hour diet to change their entire physical being. And that's why they fail and the industry is so big.

I'm using diet & exercise to illustrate a point that there is no quick fix for anything and you probably don't need any more information. What you do need is long term commitment to change. Commitment is the secret weapon that needs to come from within you.

You already know what you have to do to change any aspect of your life so commit today to doing so.

"You need to make a commitment, and once you make it, then life will give you some answers."

-Les Brown

For You, From Me

Date: _____

Thoughts_____
_____
_____
_____
_____
_____

Action_____
_____
_____
_____
_____
_____

Learn_____
_____
_____
_____
_____
_____

Conventional Wisdom

Are you living your life according to conventional wisdom?

Doing or acting in a certain way because it fits within the box of 'the usual.' If everyone lived according to conventional wisdom then the following would never had happened.

Conventional wisdom = No automobiles

Conventional wisdom = No airplanes

Conventional wisdom = No space program

Conventional wisdom = No organ transplants

This list could go on for pages.

Stop relegating yourself to being constrained by conventional wisdom. As you can see by the items on the preceding list, conventional wisdom is very often just wrong and based on outdated information.

Conventional wisdom will happily provide you with all the reasons you cannot and will not do something. Pay careful attention to your thoughts and actions so you can see how much of what you're doing is just because you've accepted the path of conventional wisdom.

"Swim upstream. Go the other way. Ignore the conventional wisdom."
-Sam Walton

For You, From Me

Date: _____

Thoughts_____

_____
_____
_____
_____
_____

Action_____

_____
_____
_____
_____
_____

Learn_____

_____
_____
_____
_____
_____

What Are You Waiting For?

What are you waiting for?

Are you waiting for the perfect moment, just the right time, or for all the stars to align before you take the steps you know you need to take to get what you want in life?

A close friend shared this story with me. He was sitting in his living room early one morning meditating in the dark when his six year old son walked in and sat in his lap. His son having all the innocence that young children do looked up and asked him "dad, what are you waiting for?" The question asked by his son gave him goosebumps because he had in fact been contemplating some major changes in his life but he had delayed in taking action.

So today I ask you, what are you waiting for?

The time will never be more perfect than now to start whatever you're waiting to start. It could be a project, job, healthier lifestyle, writing, drawing, dancing, business, relationship etc. There will never be a better time. So now ask yourself, 'what am I waiting for?'

"If we wait until we're ready, we'll be waiting for the rest of our lives."
-Lemony Snicket

For You, From Me

Date: _____

Thoughts _____
_____
_____
_____
_____
_____

Action _____
_____
_____
_____
_____
_____

Learn _____
_____
_____
_____
_____
_____

You Are Ignorant

You are ignorant!

There, I said it. Now before you begin to shower me with profanities, let me explain.

But before I explain I ask, do you know the real meaning of the word ignorant? Do you know at its core the meaning of ignorant is lacking in knowledge or training?

Children are ignorant and it's often been said that ignorance is bliss. So why then the negative feelings around ignorance? I'll tell you why. Because you don't want people to know that you don't know. But you can't know everything, can you?

Admitting to being ignorant is a fantastic place to be because you can only go up from there. In fact being a 'know it all' is the worst place to be because then you have no room, motivation or desire to grow.

So, wear your ignorance proudly and use it to your advantage. Admit when you don't know about something and use your ignorance as a spring board of opportunity to learn and explore. Soon enough the know it alls will wish they were as ignorant as you.

"The doorstep to the temple of wisdom is a knowledge of our own ignorance."
-Benjamin Franklin

For You, From Me

Date: _____

Thoughts_____

_____

_____

_____

_____

_____

Action_____

_____

_____

_____

_____

_____

Learn_____

_____

_____

_____

_____

_____

Mistakes

What unintentional mistake are you going to make today?

Are you going to give an incorrect answer, take a wrong turn, or break something you're working on?

Many life changing innovations are the results of mistakes people have made. They attempted to do one thing and as a result of an error in the process they ended up with something totally different. Studies show that successful people actually tend to be more accepting of mistakes because they know it takes many different approaches to eventually succeed at any endeavor.

Allowing yourself to be more tolerant with your mistakes will give you the courage over time to try different approaches to challenges and problems. So don't beat yourself up when you make a mistake but take the opportunity to learn from it.

At least you know what not to do next time you're in the same situation.

"A person who never made a mistake never tried anything new."
–Albert Einstein

For You, From Me

Date: _____

Thoughts_____
_____
_____
_____
_____
_____

Action_____
_____
_____
_____
_____
_____

Learn_____
_____
_____
_____
_____
_____

80% Silk 20% Cotton

What are your labels and how did you get them?

Are they self-imposed or are you living up or down to the labels people have given you?

I was given so many labels as a child and decided that since that's how the world saw me then I had to behave accordingly. Of course as a child I didn't realize that those labels were only the perspective of people around me, not how I had to be or live.

The labels people give you and you give yourself are like cake pans and you are the batter. If you have any familiarity with baking then you know that the batter will take the shape of almost any pan you put it in and eventually harden in that shape.

What shape have you taken because of labels? Are they allowing you to live a happy fulfilled life, or a small, guarded existence?

Unlike the clothing label that states factually what a garment is made from, you have the choice to create your own labels. Choose wisely.

"Life isn't about finding yourself. Life is about creating yourself."
-George Bernard Shaw

For You, From Me

Date: _____

Thoughts_____

_____
_____
_____
_____
_____

Action_____

_____
_____
_____
_____
_____

Learn_____

_____
_____
_____
_____

Something from Nothing

When was the last time you made something from nothing?

A drawing, painting, writing or even craft work from things lying around your house.

As humans we are all born with the ability to create but the majority of people stifle their creativity because they are quick to judge their creations. They also fear the judgment of others so when asked about creativity they respond with 'I'm just not the creative type.'

The ability to be creative taps in to feeling of having an abundance mindset; it gives you a confidence that you have the ability to create from nothing, so there is always more. Being creative lends itself to endless possibilities.

Give yourself some time each week to be creative. Draw, doodle, paint, write or just make something.

You don't have to share your projects with anyone, but if you do then you might just encourage them to create too.

"Don't think. Thinking is the enemy of creativity. It's self-conscious, and anything self-conscious is lousy. You can't try to do things. You simply must do things."
-Ray Bradbury

For You, From Me

Date: _____

Thoughts_____
_____
_____
_____
_____
_____

Action_____
_____
_____
_____
_____

Learn_____
_____
_____
_____
_____
_____

I Don't Want To, But...

How many sound familiar to you?

I don't want to be mean, but...
I don't want to rude, but...
I don't want to be sad, but...
I don't want to be upset, but...
I don't want to be negative, but...
I don't want to be unhealthy, but...
But, but, but...

If you know how you don't want to act then find ways to combat your behavior.

You already know what it takes to be the person you do want to be, so stop being a victim to your 'but,' bury your excuses and become the one you do.

"Most people don't have that willingness to break bad habits. They have a lot of excuses and they talk like victims."
-Carlos Santana

For You, From Me

Date: _____

Thoughts _____
_____
_____
_____
_____
_____

Action _____
_____
_____
_____
_____
_____

Learn _____
_____
_____
_____
_____
_____

Weed, Water, Wait and Repeat

You might recognize the title of this post as the gardener's manifesto; however these are the same steps you need to take if you want to achieve any large goal or change in your life.

Weed. Once you set out on a journey to accomplish anything you will start to doubt yourself and if you make your goal public then you will have others doubt and question your ability too. You will need to constantly remove the weeds of self-doubt from your mind because if you don't then they will very quickly take over.

Water. This is the life force, the nourishment that you will have to actively seek out to grow your mind. Water is the resources, people, books, information etc. that you will need to apply on a consistent basis in order to create change and achieve your goals.

Wait. This is patience you will need to have as you are on your journey. You see huge trees around you every day but do you ever see them grow? The magic of the tree happens from the inside out and this applies to you too. The magic of change will happen in your mind first and then it will manifest itself in your life.

Repeat. If you're committed to achieving your goal then you will need to perform these steps on a continuous basis, and you can't skip anyone of them.

The gardener's manifesto is a simple yet effective tool to create the change you want in your life.

"Your mind is like a garden, unless you cultivate flowers, weeds will flourish."
-Brian Tracy

Date: _____

Thoughts_____
_____
_____
_____
_____

Action_____
_____
_____
_____
_____

Learn_____
_____
_____
_____
_____

Stuff

How much stuff do you need?

Is your closest overflowing with clothes you haven't worn in years?

Do you have cabinets so full that you don't even remember what's in them?

Why?

Why do you do this?

Is it because you might wear them, or might need something from one of those cabinets?

Everything you own owns a piece of you. You have traded time, money and thought for everything you own. So take a look around your home and think about how much you have really spent and if it was worth the tradeoff.

The continuous accumulation of stuff has also been correlated with a scarcity mindset. A mindset of what if you need it one day? Or, what if you miss the opportunity to acquire it again? Neither one of these questions allow you to feel fulfilled or content.

So the next time you are considering adding to your existing stuff, take moment to ask how much value is this item really going to add to my life. And perhaps consider trading or getting rid of some stuff before you bring new stuff home.

"Let's be cautious about relying so much on material things that we have no energy left for the spiritual aspects of our lives."

-James A. Forbes

For You, From Me

Date: _____

Thoughts_____
_____
_____
_____
_____
_____

Action_____
_____
_____
_____
_____

Learn_____
_____
_____
_____
_____

The You of Tomorrow

Are the choices you make today going to result in the person you want to be tomorrow?

If yes then carry on as you are, but if not then perhaps it's time to do something different.

You can be the person you want to be by behaving that way today, regardless of how the world sees you. Your path to changing who you are starts from a small kernel of thought that will eventually grow in to action.

Start focusing on who you want to be known as, how you want to be seen and how you want to feel. Write down a list of adjectives that describe the kind of person you want be and think about the behaviors associated with your words. And then behave accordingly.

Your new behavior will seem strange at first and it's because your brain and body will be experiencing change, but over time it will become second nature and you will become your 'you of tomorrow.'

"You must begin to think of yourself as becoming the person you want to be."

-David Viscott

For You, From Me

Date: _____

Thoughts_____
_____
_____
_____
_____
_____

Action_____
_____
_____
_____
_____
_____

Learn_____
_____
_____
_____
_____
_____

Fingers Crossed

Is having your fingers crossed your strategy for getting the things you want?

I know this sounds ridiculous but it really is how many people operate. They hope that somehow, something will magically happen that will make them happier, healthier, wealthier and whatever other 'ier' they want in their lives.

Nothing you want in your life is just going to happen, even if you wait long enough. You have to be the catalyst, the reason for the things, both emotional and physical to appear in your life.

Study and research the things in life you want so that you learn how to bring them in to existence. And resolve today to uncross your fingers and commit to making a plan to creating the life you want.

"Some people want it to happen, some wish it would happen, others make it happen."

-Michael Jordan

For You, From Me

Date: _____

Thoughts_____
_____
_____
_____
_____
_____

Action_____
_____
_____
_____
_____
_____

Learn_____
_____
_____
_____
_____
_____

The Mover Advantage

Are you familiar with the phrase 'first mover advantage?'

Essentially what it means is that if you have a product or service and are first to market it with then you have an advantage because you have little or no competition.

There's also a 'second mover advantage' which you might have heard of. In this case you get to learn from the market leader, copy what they did well and beat them at their own game. It's also known as the second mouse gets the cheese because the first mouse got smacked by the mousetrap.

And yes, there's even a 'last mover advantage.' This is where there have been so many improvements that the last mover can take advantage of all the combined learnings and save time and money from avoiding the mistakes that the first and second movers have committed.

However, there is not a 'no mover advantage.' And you might think this is obvious, but how much are you moving towards what you want? Are you actively taking steps physically and mentally to gain your advantage or are you sitting, stagnant, waiting?

Start moving today towards the life you want. Make a plan and work on it. Move, move, move and you'll see the advantages come your way.

"Life is never stagnation. It is constant movement, un-rhythmic movement, as we as constant change. Things live by moving and gain strength as they go."

-Bruce Lee

For You, From Me

Date: _____

Thoughts_____
_____
_____
_____
_____
_____

Action_____
_____
_____
_____
_____
_____

Learn_____
_____
_____
_____
_____
_____

Be Grateful

What can you be grateful for today?

Actively seeking opportunities to be grateful can shift your entire perspective about your day, especially if you learn to be grateful for the little things in your life, the ones you usually take for granted.

Be grateful for things like running hot water and electricity on demand because there are still billions of people that don't have reliable or in some cases any access to these luxuries.

Be grateful for your health. Even if you do suffer from the occasional ailment, the fact that you are alive and still experience life is definitely something to be grateful for.

Be grateful for family, friends or any other relationships that add to your life.

Being grateful allows you to build a foundation of positive feelings for all that you currently have and experience. Begin to actively practice gratitude and you will find that it will help you deal with the challenges and problems you face in everyday life

"Acknowledging the good that you already have in your life is the foundation for all abundance."
-Eckhart Tolle

Date: _____

Thoughts_____
_____
_____
_____
_____
_____

Action_____
_____
_____
_____
_____
_____

Learn_____
_____
_____
_____
_____
_____

Your Natural Gifts

What are you really good at? I mean so good at it that people tell you that you're good, or they say that they wish they were as good as you at this one particular thing.

Do you embrace what they say or do you discount or negate it as anyone can do it?

More than likely you have a handful of skills that come to you naturally; these are your natural talents, your gifts. However, because they are second nature to you, you take them for granted and assume that everyone has them too. So you neglect to leverage them for your benefit.

Somewhere in the world there are successful people that have similar gifts as you and the only difference between them and you is that they have learned how to leverage and ultimately capitalize on their natural gifts.

Make a list of things that people have told you that you're good at and identify the ones that come the easiest to you. These are your natural gifts and you should spend time improving them because then you can design your life around doing what you're good at.

"The meaning of life is to find your gift. The purpose of life is to give it away."

-Pablo Picasso

For You, From Me

Date: _____

Thoughts_____
_____
_____
_____
_____
_____

Action_____
_____
_____
_____
_____
_____

Learn_____
_____
_____
_____
_____
_____

Handling Pressure and Stress

How do you handle pressure? The pressure that comes from dealing with relationships, work, finances etc. can sometimes feel overwhelming, especially if you're the kind of person that tends to combine them all in your head as one big ball.

However, pressure and stress are a natural part of the growth cycle. Everything you see in nature that has existed over time has undergone tremendous amounts of pressure and stress. Pressure and stress are the twin forces that have been responsible for the fittest and the most adaptable to continue to survive and thrive.

Journaling can be a great way to deal with stress because you're able to get the things that are causing you stress out of your head and on to paper, which can very often lead to giving you a new perspective on your problems and lead to new solutions.

The twins are never going to go away they will just change over time depending on your stage in life. So, instead of wishing that you have less pressure, it's wiser to spend your time developing coping mechanisms that can help you deal with it.

"Don't wish it were easier, wish you were better."
-Jim Rohn

For You, From Me

Date: _____

Thoughts_____
_____
_____
_____
_____

Action_____
_____
_____
_____
_____

Learn_____
_____
_____
_____
_____
_____

Energy for You

Where will you spend your energy today?

Will you spend it on things that really matter to you or will you give it away to every request and distraction that comes your way?

The majority of people remain in a reactive state just waiting for the next demand on their energy until they're too tired to do anything else and they're off to sleep. If at the end of the day you took a few minutes just to evaluate how you spent your energy you'd probably see that very little of it was actually spent on you.

Taking just a little time out throughout the day to focus your energy on yourself will give you sense of control over your own life, and can also prevent you from feeling like a victim of circumstance.

Make it a daily practice to carve out a few minutes during the day to focus your energy on what you're doing and how you're feeling. After all, it is your energy so shouldn't you spend some of it on you?

"Passion is energy. Feel the power that comes from focusing on what excites you."

-Oprah Winfrey

For You, From Me

Date: _____

Thoughts_____
_____
_____
_____
_____
_____

Action_____
_____
_____
_____
_____
_____

Learn_____
_____
_____
_____
_____
_____

Give More

Will owning one more thing really alter the trajectory of your life?

If you gave away some of what you currently own could it change someone else's life?

Owning possessions just beyond what you need is understandable because it provides a sense of security, but when you get to the point where you no longer remember or even use what you currently own then perhaps it's an opportunity to ask yourself if you really need more.

Creating a practice of continuous contribution will not only help you declutter your home, it helps shape your identity as a person that is also willing to give to others. Contribution can give you a deeper fulfillment that buying rarely does.

Make a regular practice giving away things you no longer need or use. Take a step today and find 3 things that someone else could use and give them away. Your home and your mind will feel better for it.

"Remember that the happiest people are not those getting more, but those giving more."
-H. Jackson Brown, Jr.

Date: _____

Thoughts _____

_____
_____
_____
_____
_____

Action _____

_____
_____
_____
_____
_____

Learn _____

_____
_____
_____
_____
_____

Anger

How much time do you spend being angry?

How do you justify the length of time for your anger? Do you have an equation in your head that tells you to stay angry for a minute, day or even years based on the thing that made you angry?

Anger is a funny thing because although it is a healthy emotion and there is a reason for its existence, staying angry indicates that you are either re-living the incident that made you angry or thinking about an event that might happen in the future.

If you choose to continually re-live events from the past then I strongly suggest you choose the ones that made you happy. For no other reason than they are better for your overall well-being. And if you're choosing to be angry about something that might happen in the future, well that's as ridiculous as it sounds.

Grab a pen and paper and make a list of all the reasons you're angry at a person or event. Now eat the list!

Just kidding! Study the list and ask yourself if there might be other ways to express how you're feeling or even if it's worth spending any more of your energy being angry.

"You will not be punished for your anger, you will be punished by your anger."
-Buddha

For You, From Me

Date: _____

Thoughts_____
_____
_____
_____
_____
_____

Action_____
_____
_____
_____
_____
_____

Learn_____
_____
_____
_____
_____
_____

Show Yourself

Do you tolerate other people's crappy behavior just so that they'll invite you back? Do you make excuse for why you don't speak up just so that you they'll think you're one of them? Do you pretend to be one of them when you know deep down that you're not? Why?

Why do you keep pretending to be someone you're not? Are you afraid you'll be alone?

Pretending to be someone you're not is going to tear you apart. You're going to continuously struggle to balance your multiple personalities. So the sooner you stop the easier your life will be.

Take a stand for you who are and for what you believe. At first you might not get invited back by the people you thought were your friends, but over time you'll find people that want and love for the real you to show up. You'll build relationships on you who you are. You'll find your tribe.

Make commitment today to start sharing more of who you really are and to stop hiding behind the fear of being rejected. You might be surprised at just how many people want more of the real you.

"It takes courage to grow up and become who you really are."
-E.E. Cummings

For You, From Me

Date: _____

Thoughts_____
_____
_____
_____
_____
_____

Action_____
_____
_____
_____
_____

Learn_____
_____
_____
_____
_____
_____

Seed of Thought

Have you ever had your thoughts controlled by someone else?

Well today I'm going to take over a small part of your brain. For some of you it's going to be only for a few hours but for the rest of you it's going to be for a long time. I'm giving you fair warning, so you can stop reading now or continue at your own risk.

Ok, are you ready? From this moment on **every time you see a Silver car you are going to smile.**

That's it, I'm done. I have now planted a seed in your brain that quite possibly will live in your brain forever. Years from now you when you see a silver car you will find yourself smiling and not quite remember why.

Now you might be curious as to why I did this to you. And the answer is that I want you be aware of all the information you expose yourself to and how many people with bad intentions are also planting seeds and ideas in your brain. Also how vulnerable your brain is to being influenced.

Today as you're out and about smiling at silver cars think about the other sources of information you expose yourself to how your thoughts are being influenced.

"More than anything you guard, protect your mind, for life flows from it."

-Proverbs 4:23

For You, From Me

Date: _____

Thoughts_____
_____
_____
_____
_____
_____

Action_____
_____
_____
_____
_____

Learn_____
_____
_____
_____
_____

What Matters to You?

What would you do if you could spend your time today doing anything you wanted to? If you had no demands on your time from work or family obligations what would you do today? Indulge me for a minute and think about it.

Those of you that did spend a minute thinking about it will experience a slight yet beneficial boost in your mood and energy levels. And those of you that didn't play along should really ask yourselves, why not? After all, I only asked you to commit a minute of your time to think about something that would make you happy and is important to you.

If you cannot commit to 60 seconds to think about what you would like to do with your time then it really is time to re-evaluate your life. Because, any real inspiration you feel in your life is going to be based on you thinking about how you want to spend your time.

I know that deep down you want your time and ultimately your life to matter, because most people do. So please do take that minute I asked for earlier to think about what you would do with your time because at the root of those thoughts you will find what matters to you.

"Living a life that matters doesn't happen by accident. It's not a matter of circumstance but of choice. Choose to live a life that matters."
-Michael Josephson

For You, From Me

Date: _____

Thoughts_____
_____
_____
_____
_____
_____

Action_____
_____
_____
_____
_____
_____

Learn_____
_____
_____
_____
_____
_____

I'm Proud of You

When was the last time you told someone that you're proud of them?

When was the last time someone told you that they are proud of you?

Well, today I'm telling you that I'm proud of you.

I'm proud of you for showing up and doing your best.

I'm proud of you for taking care of yourself.

I'm proud of you for being such a great friend.

I'm proud of you for working so hard.

I'm proud of you for the way you handle the bad times and for the way you create the good ones.

Close your eyes and imagine for a moment that a person you love is whispering in your ear how proud they are of you. How does it feel to hear those words being said to you? If it feels good then take the opportunity to pass those feelings along by telling someone else how proud you are of them.

"I'm proud of you."
–Me to you

For You, From Me

Date: _____

Thoughts_____
_____
_____
_____
_____
_____

Action_____
_____
_____
_____
_____

Learn_____
_____
_____
_____
_____

Your DNA

Do you know that the first humans that settled in South America walked there from Asia?

They walked across the original Siberian land bridge that connected the continents and made their way south. And you share the same DNA as those first humans.

You also share the same DNA as the humans that set sail from distant shores and made their way sailing around the world, often spending months in the search of new land.

You share the same DNA as the people that came together to put a man on the moon.

People just like you have beaten all odds and overcome tremendous obstacles to reach destinations they never knew were possible.

Your DNA contain seeds of greatness and can take you places you that you can't even imagine are possible, if?

If you let it. If you let your DNA live up to its potential it will perform miracles. So, unshackle your DNA. Let it live, let it explore, let it drive you forward.

"Exploration is really the essence of the human spirit."
-Frank Borman

For You, From Me

Date: _____

Thoughts_____
_____
_____
_____
_____
_____

Action_____
_____
_____
_____
_____
_____

Learn_____
_____
_____
_____
_____
_____

The End Comes After the Beginning

Do you ever just want to be done with something, but you haven't even started it yet?

Do you imagine the end of a project, a goal reached, something important finally completed but you haven't taken the first step to doing so?

We all want feel that sense of accomplishment, but we can't until we start.

The reason the end comes after the beginning is because that is the natural order of things. You have to go from 1 to 2, and 2 is twice as much as 1 so the effort required to getting there is also twice as much. But sometimes when you take the first step the sheer momentum can sometimes carry you forward to the next step.

Sometimes your small steps will seem trivial and small, almost as if they are half steps, but the compound effect of your small steps will accumulate over time.

Take a half step today towards one of your goals or projects that you've been thinking about doing. You might feel a little unnatural or even scared at first but the minute you take your first step you will no longer be the person you were yesterday.

"The journey of a thousand miles begins with one step."
-Lao Tzu

For You, From Me

Date: _____

Thoughts_____
_____
_____
_____
_____
_____

Action_____
_____
_____
_____
_____
_____

Learn_____
_____
_____
_____
_____
_____

Measuring Progress

How do you measure progress?

This was a question someone asked me and my response was that progress can only be measured if you know where you are right now. The problem with this is that most people don't take the time to evaluate their current state. And there are reasons they don't. Some don't want to know, others think it takes too much time, while some assume that because they're moving they are progressing.

By definition progress is the movement towards a destination. So, if you don't know where you are and where you're going then progress is almost impossible to measure. Now there are times when it's okay to just wander or go on a classic 'walk about' without a destination in mind because much can be learned from those experiences too, but if you're looking for progress then you're going to need to be more specific.

Measuring progress is not hard as long as you know what you are moving towards. However, slow progress can be challenging because you need a certain degree of mental fortitude to continue on. And usually the bigger the goal or destination the slower the progress feels. Take a step today of measuring progress in one area of your life by evaluating where you are, where you'd like to be and how you'll get there.

"Make measurable progress in reasonable time."

-Jim Rohn

For You, From Me

Date: _____

Thoughts_____
_____
_____
_____
_____
_____

Action_____
_____
_____
_____
_____

Learn_____
_____
_____
_____
_____
_____

Be You

Do you ever spend any time remembering who you were as a child?

Somewhere deep inside you are the traces of the kid that believed anything was possible. There are traits that you have suppressed because you were told you had to become an adult. You had to fit the mold that others designed for you.

Some of the traits that you have suppressed are your natural given abilities and you never allowed them to ever come to fruition. Because for whatever reason, whether external or internal you decided that those traits would not be accepted or would not be beneficial in adulthood. The unfortunate thing is that at your core those traits, like weeds will always be trying to surface and you will spend your entire life fighting them. So why not embrace them?

What were those things that you enjoyed doing so much as a child that the world could have stopped and you wouldn't have noticed? The desire to do those activities are still somewhere inside you.

Make a list today of all the things you used to enjoy doing, you'll see that it probably isn't a very long list. Choose one of the activities and find a way to incorporate it back into your life. I guarantee that when you do you'll find yourself grinning from ear to ear just like you used to as a kid.

"To be yourself in a world that is constantly trying to make you something else is the greatest accomplishment."

-Ralph Waldo Emerson

For You, From Me

Date: _____

Thoughts_____
_____
_____
_____
_____
_____

Action_____
_____
_____
_____
_____
_____

Learn_____
_____
_____
_____
_____
_____

Build More Relationships

Do you actively build relationships with people or do you wait for them to happen by chance? Over the years the word networking has taken on a negative connotation, but that's because most approach it in a transactional, 'what's in it for me?' mentality.

Relationships with people are really everything we have and connecting with people is what we are naturally driven to do. However, in today's digital age so many have a better relationship with their screens than they do with the people around them. They've come to believe that the virtual interactions are a replacement for real ones.

Actively seeking opportunities to interact in person with people can enhance your personal and professional life. It will add depth to who you are as a person because it will force you to grow as you continuously step out of what you know and are used to.

As with any new behavior actively seeking out new people to talk to takes some practice and will seem uncomfortable at first. But as you get better at it you'll realize that majority of people you meet either have, or had the same apprehension about new meeting people as you. Take an active step this week of meeting one new person, and when you do just relax and be yourself.

"Treasure your relationships, not your possessions."
-Anthony J. D'Angelo

For You, From Me

Date: _____

Thoughts _____
_____
_____
_____
_____
_____

Action _____
_____
_____
_____
_____
_____

Learn _____
_____
_____
_____
_____
_____

Stay Curious

When was the last time you researched something you were interested in?

Or tried to find out just how something worked, even if it wasn't directly related to your job?

Many have had the habit of being curious trained out of them. The repeated schooling of don't ask too many questions and don't be wrong has removed so much of the natural curiosity that humans have. The fear of being wrong has also contributed the decline in curiosity.

Maintaining a healthy amount of curiosity is a great first step to having an open mind and a growth mindset. Reading and learning about things that are unrelated to your everyday life is also a great way to stoke your curiosity. Being curious also has the benefit of moving your mind from a passive state to an active one. One in which you are asking questions.

Take some time out today to be intentionally curious. Try a new food, talk to a stranger or read about something that ordinarily you would have no interest in and ask questions, lots of questions. See what new possibilities you can discover behind your curiosity.

"I have no special talent. I am only passionately curious."
-Albert Einstein

For You, From Me

Date: _____

Thoughts_____
_____
_____
_____
_____
_____

Action_____
_____
_____
_____
_____
_____

Learn_____
_____
_____
_____
_____
_____

Instant...Results?

Do you ever feel like you're not getting what you want fast enough? You want it now, so why can't you have it now? You think you're doing all the right things but it's just taking so long, almost too long. This could apply to any area of your life.

You've been programmed by the just add water' media that your needs and wants should be instantly fulfilled. Pay attention to the messages you see and hear, how many times this week you are exposed to one or more of the following phrases.

Get rich quick

Lose weight fast

Overnight success

Over time these messages cause you to have an internal disparity in your life. You begin to feel as though there's something you're not doing right and this is the emotion these messages are designed to create. They are designed for you to act but not necessarily in your best interest.

The trick is to realize that any endeavor that is going to create lasting change in your life is going to take time. It's going to take time and effort to begin and more important, it's going to take even more effort to maintain. So allow your rational thinking mind to push your feelings of 'why don't I have it now' to the side and keep moving forward.

"If you can't fly then run, if you can't run then walk, if you can't walk then crawl, but whatever you do you have to keep moving forward."

—*Martin Luther King*

For You, From Me

Date: _____

Thoughts _____
_____
_____
_____
_____
_____

Action _____
_____
_____
_____
_____
_____

Learn _____
_____
_____
_____
_____
_____

Serendipitous Accidents

Are you familiar with 'accidental discoveries?'

One of the most famous is Penicillin, which according to the inventor Alexander Fleming was discovered by a serendipitous accident.

Throughout history there have been many other serendipitous accidents that have created many of the products you take for granted today.

Corn Flakes for a clean healthy diet.

The Slinky was supposed to hold equipment on naval ships.

Coca-Cola was supposed to be a medical remedy.

Post-it Notes were supposed to be a super adhesive.

Potato chips were the result of an angry chef.

Play-Doh was supposed to be wallpaper cleaner.

These are just a few, but you can find many more that are now multi-million if not billion dollar products.

The thing about serendipitous accidents is that you have to be continuously creating and experimenting for the accident to happen.

Now there's no guarantee that you'll have the next million dollar idea but the next time you find yourself using a product in a way that is not what it was designed for, ask yourself, is this a serendipitous accident?

"There'll always be serendipity involved in discovery."
-Jeff Bezos

Date: _____

Thoughts_____
_____
_____
_____
_____
_____

Action_____
_____
_____
_____
_____
_____

Learn_____
_____
_____
_____
_____
_____

The Perfect Age

What is the perfect age?

When are you too young to be taken seriously?
When are you too old to try something new?
What if you didn't know how old you are?

Age is a strange phenomenon because although it's measured by how much time has passed it's also measured in social context. Age is used to measure progress in life.

At 16 you should be doing this and at 21 you're allowed to do this and by 30 you should have done this and at 60, well now you're half way done and you really shouldn't be trying anything.

When you ask someone how old they are it's rarely because you're interested in the number of years they've been alive. It's so that you can mentally categorize where you think they should be in life.

I once read an interview where a woman born in remote area of the world was asked when she was born, and her reply was, in the winter. There was no context of time.

Do your thoughts about your own age hold you back?

If you look hard enough you will find examples of people from all ages accomplishing all kinds of things that they 'shouldn't be able to' at their age.

What if today you dismissed your belief about age and explored all the things you want to do? Who knows, you might just be the perfect age.

"None are so old as those who have outlived enthusiasm."
-Henry David Thoreau

Date: _____

Thoughts _____
_____
_____
_____
_____

Action _____
_____
_____
_____
_____

Learn _____
_____
_____
_____
_____
_____

I Disagree

I strongly disagree with what you said!

Let me rephrase.
I vehemently disagree with you!
I emphatically disagree with you!
What do you mean, let you finish!
I already know I don't like what you're going to say.
No! I won't give you chance to share your thoughts or ideas.
Yes, I know you just started to speak but it doesn't matter.
I've already decided you're wrong.
No! I don't need more time to think about it. In my mind seconds are like hours.
In fact, my response is chambered and ready to go before you even open your mouth.
...Why don't you talk to me anymore?
If any of this sounds familiar then you might be suffering from a disease known as Closed Mindedness.

Fortunately for you there is a cure and the cure doesn't mean you have to agree with everyone. It does mean giving people the opportunity to share their thoughts and allowing yourself time to process what you hear. Who knows, your actions might prompt them to listen to you too.

"You can disagree without being disagreeable."
-Ruth Bader Ginsburg

For You, From Me

Date: _____

Thoughts_____
_____
_____
_____
_____
_____

Action_____
_____
_____
_____
_____
_____

Learn_____
_____
_____
_____
_____
_____

Uninterrupted Time

How much uninterrupted time can you make for yourself today?

Can you step away from the internet for 20 minutes?

Can you put down your phone for 20 minutes?

Can you find a quiet spot to think for 20 minutes?

What can you do to clear 20 minutes for yourself?

Constantly bombarding your mind with input is like standing at a buffet gorging on food without any end in sight. Sounds ridiculous and hopefully you'd never engage in such an activity, so why do it to your mind.

If the idea of stepping away for 20 minutes makes you nervous and you're already making excuses in your head as to why you can't, then that should tell you something about your addiction to constant stimulation.

It's just 20 minutes. That's less than 2% of your entire day.

Your brain deserves it.

You can do it.

"The best cure for the body is a quiet mind."
-Napoleon Bonaparte

For You, From Me

Date: _____

Thoughts _____
_____
_____
_____
_____
_____

Action _____
_____
_____
_____
_____
_____

Learn _____
_____
_____
_____
_____
_____

Blank Canvas

Have you ever stared at a blank canvas and wondered what to draw?

Have you spent time staring at a blank sheet of paper as you struggle with what to write?

Perhaps for you it's the first words of a speech or presentation that have you stumped?

It's not the question of where to start that paralyzes most people.

It's the thought of, what if I get it wrong. What if the first line I draw or the first words I write are bad.

It's the intimidation of working without instructions, aka constraints.

Life would be so much easier if every time you started a new project a magic fairy could just tell you what to do, but then the ideas would be theirs and not yours.

Seeking inspiration from other people's work is great and can be helpful, but also learn to trust your own intuition and ideas.

Find the courage you had when you were a child, draw your first line and write your first word. Be proud that you've started and don't worry if it's not 'good.' You can always start again.

"You don't have to be great to start, but you have to start to be great."
-Zig Ziglar

For You, From Me

Date: _____

Thoughts_____
_____
_____
_____
_____
_____

Action_____
_____
_____
_____
_____
_____

Learn_____
_____
_____
_____
_____
_____

Discrepancy Syndrome

Do you suffer from discrepancy syndrome? Wait! You've never heard of it?

I'm surprised that you haven't because it's so common.

Discrepancy syndrome is when you wish something is different than it really is.

You may have heard of it by its other names, anger and frustration.

Every incident of anger and frustration is caused by wishing that the situation at hand is different than it really is.

The good news about discrepancy syndrome is that there is a cure; the bad news is that you have to cure yourself.

You have to decide how long you will continue to dwell in the moments of discrepancy that are occurring or that have passed.

This is not to say that you shouldn't experience anger or frustration because they can both be great self-motivators for change.

But for how long?

There's a great Buddhist saying that the first arrow causes the pain but then we choose to shoot ourselves with a second arrow, and this causes the suffering, which is optional.

So the next time you find yourself angry or frustrated see if you can learn to separate how you feel from what is occurring. Who knows? You might just cure yourself of discrepancy syndrome.

For You, From Me

"For every minute you remain angry, you give up sixty seconds of peace of mind."
-Ralph Waldo Emerson

Date: _____

Thoughts_____
_____
_____
_____
_____

Action_____
_____
_____
_____
_____

Learn_____
_____
_____
_____
_____

Your Emotions

Are you in tune with your emotions?

Do you spend time listening to your emotions?

Your emotions are like a barometer, thermometer, speedometer and any other kind of 'meter' all wrapped up in one instrument. They are designed to guide you and even in some cases to keep you alive.

Your entire day is filled with a variety of emotions and you are constantly riding the waves of how you feel. And those feelings drive your actions.

Tracking your emotions can be an interesting experiment. You might find that you reach for food when you're upset or make phone calls when you're happy or a myriad of other behaviors.

The ability to observe your emotions without always immediately reacting to them can be a very powerful skill because it can ultimately change your entire life.

"Take control of your consistent emotions and begin to consciously and deliberately reshape your daily experience of life."

-Tony Robbins

For You, From Me

Date: _____

Thoughts _____
_____
_____
_____
_____
_____

Action _____
_____
_____
_____
_____

Learn _____
_____
_____
_____
_____

Good News, Bad News

Have you ever tried getting in shape?

Or, have you ever tried your hand at growing a plant?

At first glance these two activities might not seem to have anything in common, but they do.

You see, the good news is that you can start to get in shape or grow a plant, but the bad news is that you can never stop, because if you stop then it's over. You will very quickly be out of shape and the plant will die.

Any endeavor you set out on has impermanence built into it. Whether it's a relationship you're trying to cultivate or grow a business, both require continuous attention.

There is always a level of excitement that comes with starting something new and never a shortage people encouraging you to do so. However, keep in mind that although many have spoken about the difficulty of starting something, very few share just how much effort is required to keep going.

So the next time you're thinking about starting a new project remember the good news, bad news equation, because your first step will be followed by a million more.

"There's a difference between knowing the path and walking the path."

-Morpheus, The Matrix

For You, From Me

Date: _____

Thoughts _____
_____
_____
_____
_____
_____

Action _____
_____
_____
_____
_____
_____

Learn _____
_____
_____
_____
_____
_____

A Key to Learning

Do you know that there is a short yet powerful phrase that you can learn which is both liberating and empowering?

It's a phrase that you've probably said before, but with hesitation.

It's a phrase that when used correctly can be your springboard to learning and opening your mind to new opportunities.

However, this phrase requires you to be confident. It requires you to be humble.

It will be obvious once you see it, but when you do, don't just read it, say it out loud.

Are you ready?

Wait! First a quick promise between me and you that you will say it out loud.

Okay, here' goes.

Say, 'I don't know' out loud.

Did you do it?

How did it feel?

Admitting to not knowing is your opportunity to learn.

I know that there are times when you feel like you're expected to know everything and it's very easy to pretend that you do, but the reality is that none of us have all the answers.

So the next time you're asked a question and you don't have the answer, admit to not knowing and follow it up with, but

I can find out. Not only will you find this freeing, you will also find that you will be more open to trying new things.

"Being at ease with not knowing is crucial for answers to come to you."
-Eckhart Tolle

Date:_____

Thoughts_____
_____
_____
_____
_____

Action_____
_____
_____
_____
_____

Learn_____
_____
_____
_____

Mindless Accumulation

What do you have that you don't need?

Why do you have it?

Why does it occupy space in your home?

Do you keep it 'just in case?' How many times has there been a 'just in case' when you've needed to use it?

The mindless accumulation of things is a symptom of a deeper problem. Mindless accumulation is tied directly to temporary, in the moment happiness. If you think about it you will realize that that a thing, an inanimate object rarely holds the power to give you happiness. If it did then every time you walked into your home everything you owned would make you happy.

There are probably a handful of items that provide pleasant memories but most of what you own just takes up physical space and even worse, sometimes it even occupies your mental space.

The constant need to possess is a vicious cycle because ultimately you become owned by your possessions. So, the next time you feel the need to buy one more thing, really ask yourself, why am I buying this and what need am I looking to fulfill?

Perhaps you'll end up with less stuff but more answers.

"The things you own end up owning you."
-Tyler Durden

For You, From Me

Date: _____

Thoughts_____
_____
_____
_____
_____
_____

Action_____
_____
_____
_____
_____
_____

Learn_____
_____
_____
_____
_____
_____

Take a Break from Media

When was the last time you unplugged from all media?

I mean nothing at all.

No TV, radio or social media? Do you think you can unplug, even for half a day? If not, what does that tell you about yourself?

You see, media only has one goal. To sell you stuff. And they do this by providing you 'news and information' that focuses on two ends of the spectrum, bad news and good news. The bad news is to create fear and urgency and the good news creates envy and questions about your own life.

Boring news about people's everyday lives would never capture an audience because it can't be sensationalized. And this constant exposure to bad news and good news drives your mind to constantly compare your life to the life of others. It's a continuous; my life is better than or worse than conversation. Even though the majority of the time this conversation is happening subconsciously for you, it's still happening.

Consider the act of taking a break from media a fast for your mind. Providing your brain a break from the constant bombardment can give you the opportunity to think and listen to what you have to say instead always listening to the thoughts of others.

"Constantly exposing yourself to popular culture and the mass media will ultimately shape your reality tunnel in ways that are not necessarily conducive to achieving your Soul Purpose and Life Calling."

-Anthon St. Maarten

Date: _____

Thoughts_____
_____
_____
_____

Action_____
_____
_____
_____

Learn_____
_____
_____
_____

Random Act of Kindness

Have you ever performed a random act of kindness? If you have, then do you remember how it made you feel? And if you haven't, then great because today's your day to do so.

Performing a random act of kindness doesn't have to cost a lot of time or money. It doesn't even require much planning, but it does require some intentionality. It does require you to look for or think about situations that allow for the 'random' act.

Here are some ideas that might help you.

Send a handwritten note to someone

Pay for the person behind you in a store or restaurant

Over tip a server

Email a friend or acquaintance expressing appreciation

Pay a genuine compliment to someone

There are many more ideas that you can find on the web, or you can be creative and come up with your own. Pick one today and do it. I'm sure you'll find that the random act of kindness will probably brighten your day more than the person you did the act for.

"Carry out a random act of kindness, with no expectation of reward, safe in the knowledge that one day someone might do the same for you."
-Princess Diana

For You, From Me

Date: _____

Thoughts_____
_____
_____
_____
_____
_____

Action_____
_____
_____
_____
_____
_____

Learn_____
_____
_____
_____
_____
_____

A Penny for Your Thoughts

How much are your thoughts worth to you?

Have you ever considered placing a real value on your 'thinking time?' Or is your mind an open playground where other people's thoughts and ideas can come and play at will?

You've probably seen an old playground that has been rutted and worn down so much due to lack of upkeep that eventually it's no good for anyone. Well, if you keep allowing others to access your mind and your time then you too will be no good for anyone, including yourself.

Stepping away from the constant allure of conversation, distractions and the need to respond to every request of your time is hard to do because your brain loves being 'wanted,' and it doesn't want to 'miss out.'

However, if you stay constantly engaged then you can no longer pay attention to your own thoughts and if you don't place a value on your thoughts then you really can't expect others to do so.

"Thinking is the hardest work there is, which is probably the reason why so few engage in it."
-Henry Ford

For You, From Me

Date: _____

Thoughts_____
_____
_____
_____
_____
_____

Action_____
_____
_____
_____
_____

Learn_____
_____
_____
_____
_____

Make Someone's Day

When was the last time you set out to make someone's day?

I don't mean by buying them a gift but just by saying something nice or showing kindness. Looking for an opportunity to give a compliment or kind word is a quick and easy way to make someone's day.

Studies show that in some instances people that receive compliments will actually experience the same positive effect as if they had received cash. When you say a kind word or give a compliment you can sometimes see a person's eyes light up or even stand a little taller.

Giving compliments or showing kindness doesn't have to be a manufactured experience but it does have to a conscious one. It doesn't take long to do but it does take a moment to really engage with the person in front of you. To borrow loosely from the Homeland Security phrase "If you see something nice, say something nice."

"Kind words do not cost much. Yet they accomplish much."
-Blaise Pascal

For You, From Me

Date: _____

Thoughts _____

Action _____

Learn _____

FOMO

What is FOMO?

It's the Fear of Missing Out.

You know that feeling of anxiety you have when you can't go to the party that all your friends are going to, and you know that they'll all be talking about how much fun they had? Well that's FOMO

How do you get it? You have an internal emotional hole that you're looking to fill by an external activity.

How do you get rid of it? You take FOMO for a walk in to the woods and you bury it. You learn to fill your own emotional hole.

FOMO is you experiencing emotions that you might feel based on a future activity. I know, it sounds confusing and that's because it is. You see, almost everything you do is driven by how you think you might feel or the reward you'll receive once you do it.

The problem with FOMO is that it causes you to overcommit, because you don't want to miss anything. It also prevents you from being present in what you're doing because you're thinking about what you're missing.

Learn to accept the fact that you can't be everywhere and that you should thoroughly appreciate, enjoy and leverage the opportunities you do have. Remember YOLO – You Only Live Once- so why waste it living in FOMO?

"No matter what you do or where you are, you're going to be missing out on something."
-Alan Arkin

Date: _____

Thoughts_____
_____
_____
_____
_____

Action_____
_____
_____
_____
_____

Learn_____
_____
_____
_____
_____

Perspective

What is your view of the world and how do you judge people that don't see things your way?

One day while watching my 3 year old daughter walk through a crowd a thought occurred to me, that all she sees is adult butts all day long. Her entire world view is based on a 'below the waist' perspective.

We're all guilty of only seeing things our way and judging others for not seeing things from our perspective. Yet intellectually we know that if we all had the same thoughts and ideas then how boring our world would be.

Recognizing that we are constantly judging people from our perspective and then allowing for a little curiosity about why they don't see the world the way do can help broaden your perspective and also increase empathy.

So the next time you're quick to judge someone's perspective, think of my 3 year old looking at butts all day, smile and give the other person's perspective a chance.

"Everything we hear is an opinion, not a fact. Everything we see is a perspective, not the truth."

-Marcus Aurelius

For You, From Me

Date: _____

Thoughts _____
_____
_____
_____
_____
_____

Action _____
_____
_____
_____
_____

Learn _____
_____
_____
_____
_____
_____

Feeling Alive

When was the last time you felt alive?

There is a big difference in being alive and feeling alive. Being alive is what you do every day. Sitting in the same chairs, going to the same places, talking to the same people, driving the same route, eating the same food and on and on until eventually a layer of rust forms over your senses creating nothing but a dull existence, essentially being alive.

Feeling alive on the other hand is that feeling of butterflies you had when you first held hands with a person you had a crush on.

The fear you felt on the top of a rollercoaster.

The nervousness you felt when you were asked to speak in front of a group. Feeling alive comes from not knowing what will happen next, it's at this point that all of your senses are alive because biologically they have to be in order to keep you alive.

Try an activity this week that can help stimulate feelings you once experienced.

Attend an event where you don't know anyone.

Take a class in something you're interested in.

Talk or flirt with strangers.

Go to store you wouldn't normally go to.

Do something creative and then show people.

Ask the server in a restaurant what their favorite item is and try it.

For the more adventurous souls, try bungee jumping, roller skating, fencing, or dancing. Physical activities are fantastic for feeling alive because they stimulate both mind and body. You're here to experience life, so go out and do it while you still have the opportunity. Don't just be alive, feel alive!

"Most men lead lives of quiet desperation and go to the grave with the song still in them."
−Henry David Thoreau

Date: _____

Thoughts_____
_____
_____
_____

Action_____
_____
_____
_____

Learn_____
_____
_____
_____

Smiling and Dialing

If you've ever been in phone sales then you're probably familiar with the phrase 'smiling and dialing.'

The reason for smiling before you dial is that it changes your entire physiology and often the person on the other end of the line that can only hear your voice can sense that you are smiling.

Research shows that putting a big smile on your face actually triggers happiness in your brain. Smiling has also shown to improve creativity since a brain in a positive state is open to ideas, which in turn improves problem solving.

Consciously smiling during times of anger or frustration can immediately change your view on a situation. Smiling will send a message to your brain that things will be okay and perhaps aren't as serious as you think they are.

Making an effort throughout your day to smile will not only enhance your mood and well-being, but will also make you more likeable and approachable.

"We shall never know all the good that a simple smile can do."
-Mother Teresa

For You, From Me

Date: _____

Thoughts _____
_____
_____
_____
_____
_____

Action _____
_____
_____
_____
_____
_____

Learn _____
_____
_____
_____
_____
_____

Insecurity

What are your insecurities?

We all have them but rarely do we take the time to really examine them. Take some time this week to write out your insecurities and see how they are affecting your daily actions.

Some of the most common insecurities that people have are He or she might leave me if.

If don't behave a certain way then I will not be accepted.

Comparing yourself to others and then feeling less than perfect.

Criticism you received as a child still dictating how you live your life.

Listing out your insecurities will give you the opportunity to face each one and evaluate if they are grounded in reality or if they were caused by some previous experience that you have been replaying over time. The first step you can take to overcoming your insecurities is accepting and loving who you are. Having a sense of self approval doesn't mean that you don't want become better or improve, it does mean coming to terms with who you are today. Look in a mirror today and say 'I love you' to your reflection. This might sound like a silly exercise, but I guarantee you that many people cannot look themselves in the eyes and do this. Remember, if you can't love yourself, how will you make room for others to love you.

For You, From Me

"Accept who you are."
–Smart Person

Date: _____

Thoughts _____
_____
_____
_____
_____

Action _____
_____
_____
_____
_____

Learn _____
_____
_____
_____
_____

Waiting for Permission

Are you waiting for permission to do your thing?

Are you waiting for permission to take the next step?

Are you waiting for permission to be you?

Who are you waiting for permission from?

Are you afraid that you'll rock the boat or upset someone?

The truth is that you might and that's why you've decided to play it safe.

There will never be a time when you will please everybody, no matter how hard you try. I'm not saying you shouldn't care about people's feelings or disregard them, but don't use them as excuses you hold yourself back.

Give yourself permission to explore, to grow, to try, to fail, to experiment, so that you can experience your life to the fullest.

"Poor is the man whose pleasures depend on the permission of another."

-Madonna Ciccone

For You, From Me

Date: _____

Thoughts _____
_____
_____
_____
_____
_____

Action _____
_____
_____
_____
_____

Learn _____
_____
_____
_____
_____

Your Last Words?

What was will be the last thing you say today to your children as you drop them off to school, your spouse as you leave for work, your friends, your co-workers?

Will they be words of love, kindness, appreciation?

Very often we get so caught up in the trivialities of life that we forget to convey just how much those that are closest to us really mean to us. However we've become experts at conveying our negative emotions, almost automatic.

What if you really tried today to not get mad, angry, upset?

What if you knew today was your last opportunity to share your last words with the people in your life. What would suddenly become less important?

What will be your last words?

"You cannot do a kindness too soon, for you never know how soon it will be too late."

–Ralph Waldo Emerson

For You, From Me

Date: _____

Thoughts _____
_____
_____
_____
_____
_____

Action _____
_____
_____
_____
_____

Learn _____
_____
_____
_____
_____

It's Messy for Everyone

Everyone's life is a mess to some extent.

Unfortunately all you get to see is the highlight reel, a brief picture of their existence. And then you compare your entire life to the snapshot you've been exposed too. Your brain then takes the snapshot and goes in to the 'life is good for everyone but me' thought cycle.

Read the biography of any famous person you admire and you'll find that they have all experienced struggles in some area of life. Broken relationships, financial troubles, health issues, one or all of these is part of everyone's journey.

I love the example of the duck on water. All we see is the duck moving gracefully along, but if we looked under the surface we would see its feet paddling frantically to move it along.

So the next time you find yourself thinking how perfect someone's life is consider for a moment that they might be thinking the same thing about you.

"Everything has been figured out, except how to live."
–John-Paul Satre

For You, From Me

Date: _____

Thoughts_____
_____
_____
_____
_____
_____

Action_____
_____
_____
_____
_____
_____

Learn_____
_____
_____
_____
_____
_____

One Size Fits One

Are you disappointed or surprised when?

The diet and exercise program didn't' work for you.

The get rich now program didn't work for you.

The fast growth program didn't work for your company.

The 10 tips to a great relationship didn't work for you.

You see, how to's, tips and tricks are not a one size fits all solution. They are guidelines that worked for someone else in the past.

Now I'm not discounting certain fundamentals and principles that stand the test of time, what I am saying that you will have to experiment and find your own unique solutions to your challenges.

Continue to learn and take in new information to apply to your own personal endeavors, just keep in mind that you will always experience a different outcome from the one you expected.

"Always remember that you are absolutely unique. Just like everyone else."

-Margaret Mead

For You, From Me

Date: _____

Thoughts_____
_____
_____
_____
_____
_____

Action_____
_____
_____
_____
_____

Learn_____
_____
_____
_____
_____

Missing Pieces

Have you ever worked on a puzzle only to realize that some pieces are missing?

That's essentially how life is.

When you were born you were given a certain number of pieces like your gender, your parents, where you were born, and perhaps a few others but the rest of the pieces are missing. And it's now up to you to find or make the rest of the pieces.

It's up to you to determine what you want the picture your life to look like and then get to work making it a reality.

It's up to you to find the resources and develop the skills you need to complete the puzzle.

You might wish that you had all the pieces up front but that would mean that everything in your life would have been pre-determined and you wouldn't have the opportunity to create your own.

The missing pieces of your life are the ones where you get to choose what you want and how you want your life puzzle to look when it's finished.

"It takes half your life before you discover life is a do-it-yourself project."

-Napoleon Hill

For You, From Me

Date: _____

Thoughts_____
_____
_____
_____
_____
_____

Action_____
_____
_____
_____
_____
_____

Learn_____
_____
_____
_____
_____
_____

Subconscious Choices

How many subconscious choices will you make today?

Probably more than you can keep track of.

Some of your subconscious choices will be as simple as which lane to drive in and others will determine your how your live your life.

Your subconscious choices are tied directly to your beliefs and values. And your beliefs and values will drive your behavior because they will prioritize your actions.

For example, if you don't have a belief or value that says great health is extremely important then you will behave and act accordingly. And during the day your subconscious choices will be to not exercise and allow yourself excuses to eat unhealthy food.

The way to leverage your subconscious thoughts is to take the time to clearly define what is important to you. Once you bring this level of clarity to your mind then your subconscious choices will begin to drive you towards the outcomes you want.

"Whatever we plant in our subconscious mind and nourish with repetition and emotion will one day become a reality."
-Earl Nightingale

For You, From Me

Date: _____

Thoughts _____

_____
_____
_____
_____
_____

Action _____

_____
_____
_____
_____
_____

Learn _____

_____
_____
_____
_____
_____

Infinite Loop

Is your life on an infinite loop?

In the world of software development an infinite loop is when a computer program loops endlessly and occurs because certain conditions will never be met.

According to software developers the infinite loop is usually caused by a bug in the program.

Do you have a bug in your software that keeps you on an infinite loop?

For you does one day roll into another day and on and on because you haven't set any conditions to be met?

You're probably familiar with the idiom of 'stop and smell the roses,' but do you?

Do you take pause to appreciate, to think, to relax?

Knowing when to stop is just as important as knowing when to start.

Get in the habit of actively stopping, even if just for few minutes. Step away from the computer, the phone, the TV, and the continuous inputs. Give your software the opportunity to reset and stop the infinite loop.

"With mindfulness, you can establish yourself in the present in order to touch the wonders of life that are available in that moment."
-Thich Nhat Hanh

For You, From Me

Date: _____

Thoughts_____
_____
_____
_____
_____
_____

Action_____
_____
_____
_____
_____
_____

Learn_____
_____
_____
_____
_____
_____

This Is It

This is the moment that will become your remember when, and your good old days.

This is the day you dig deep and find reasons to move forward and advance your life or you decide remain on the course you're on.

This is the day you decide to do more for yourself, your community, your world.

This is the moment you decide to stop engaging in toxic relationships because you're tired of feeling the drain on your energy.

This is the moment you decide how you will define your destiny and summon the courage to pursue it, or decide to live small because you're afraid express your dreams.

This is it. It is your day, your time, and your moment. Own it. Play with it, create with it and live with it because you will never see today again. This is it.

"Carpe Diem –Enjoy, make use of and seize the day, the moment."
-Horace

For You, From Me

Date: _____

Thoughts _____
_____
_____
_____
_____
_____

Action _____
_____
_____
_____
_____
_____

Learn _____
_____
_____
_____
_____
_____

Authors Note:

Best-selling author and marketing expert Seth Godin very eloquently said that "Self-publishing is not merely a new way to get to the market. Self-publishing is the responsibility of choosing oneself. And that changes everything, completely and forever."

I have taken the responsibility of choosing myself, however I know that I cannot succeed alone. So, I'm asking for your help.

If you've enjoyed this book then you can help me out by telling your friends or purchasing additional copies for people in your network that you think would enjoy it too.

On the other hand, if you didn't like it then please let me know. I'm invested in becoming a better listener and writer and welcome your feedback.

You can reach me through my website www.rajdaniels.com or reach out to me on twitter @raj_daniels.

Intentionally,

Raj

Made in the USA
Lexington, KY
08 May 2018